OCT 2 3 2001

P9-DDG-376

THE BRITISH LIBRARY
writers' lives

Virginia Woolf

24th Aug.
1924

Monk's House
Rodmell
Lewes.

My dear Pernel,

I suppose there is no chance of your coming here this summer? It would be very nice to see you again — I can't bear only meeting on the pavement in horrible dreary dusty surroundings. How I hate funeral services! & can't feel anything at them — either for Katherine & myself, or any one else. I wish I had seen her again. Never shall I forget her at

Newnham, hundreds of years ago, & her sitting in that sheer grim room with her talking — what a satisfactory & altogether charming human being she was!

Here I am writing in my garden room, which you have never seen, spreading first my left hand & then my right over an oil stove, to dry the glutinous damp. In an hour's time, perhaps, I shall see Clive appearing over the hill. On the other hand, if it goes on raining, Leonard & I will lunch together off roast (I think) mutton; I shall tell him how I woke up in the night & thought of writing a letter to you; & also of all kinds of catastrophes which

may befall us in the coming year. We have now undertaken so many responsibilities — Wadge Ryland, a comedowned youth, is one of them; & another is Mrs Joad. Both sit in the basement at Tavistock addressing envelopes, & cheered by occasional visits from me. We discuss literature. Madies send for 20 Rectors daughters, by Miss Mayor, who may well be a friend of yours. She has the profile of Scylla & once acted Ophelia — does that convey anything to you? Where ordinary women have hair, she has brown sea weed — Lytten once had tea with her, & she hated us all, until I wrote to her in praise of her novel, when she wheeled round the other way, & now steps the world (she said) like Hallim in the sun.

I am writing great rubbish — do not blame me; for unless I do write

something, Irene will let the end of her line drop, & me go, for ever. But that true? Have you a word to urge in defence of your conduct? True, you're a great swell: at the top of your tree; magnificent; adored; & all the rest of it; but look down, my dear Pernel, into the grass, among the sunflowers, & see the lesser creatures who there abound. Myself among them.

I saw Hope the other day; but I shan't tell you what I think of her novel unless you write to me. I shan't tell you what I'm reading, writing, thinking, supposing, & inventing about my friend unless you write to me. Or it would be better still to come; but how can I suggest that. Years ago Pernel said she kept didn't visit where there weren't baths kept.

Leonard sends his love

Yr aff
VW.

THE BRITISH LIBRARY
writers' lives

Virginia Woolf

RUTH WEBB

OXFORD
UNIVERSITY PRESS

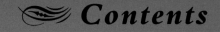 # *Contents*

☙ *Preface*

> *For she had a great variety of selves to call upon, far more than we have been able to find room for; since a biography is considered complete if it merely accounts for six or seven selves, whereas a person may well have as many thousand.*
>
> Virginia Woolf, *Orlando*

Virginia Woolf attracts some of the most diverse responses of any twentieth-century writer. At one end of the spectrum are those who vilify her as a snob and eugenicist; at the other are an adoring group who have sanctified her, seeing her suicide as a sacrifice or martyrdom. At times her detractors and acolytes alike seem uninterested in reading attentively what she wrote. Some critics have mistaken the outrageous comments of characters she created as her own views. Some enthusiasts ignore her novels and journalism, content with a fragmentary knowledge of the members of her family and her circle of friends collectively known as The Bloomsbury Group.

Much of the response to Virginia Woolf is a reaction against what she and those close to her appear to represent. The English class structure and its associated antipathies have some bearing on how she is perceived. Virginia was born into a privileged background and had a number of wealthy and titled friends. The man she married came from a different background. Leonard Woolf was a Jew who had left-wing political views, upon which he acted. Virginia supported him but was not wholly committed to some of the causes to which he gave his time and energy. She wrote articles and reviews for both left- and right-wing newspapers but, in order to be free to publish what she wished, she set up her own printing press with her husband. In addition to novels, she wrote biography, autobiographical sketches, short stories, essays and drama, as well as thousands of letters and volumes of diaries. In her diaries, she wrote frankly about her own life and the lives of her family and friends. She recognized that she occasionally contradicted herself, and she consciously gave this tendency to characters in her novels. She also used her diaries to comment on her work-in-progress, and to record her immediate responses to criticisms of her published work.

Virginia Woolf was born in Victorian England, and from an early age was aware of the unequal treatment of the sexes. She was a feminist who lived to see women win the right to vote, and her feminism became more radical as she grew older. During her lifetime, she witnessed two world wars, observing the rise of right-wing dictatorships in the 1930s. In her writing, she sought to connect the political with the personal. She declined all honours that were offered to her. When she died, more than two hundred people, from a great variety of backgrounds, wrote to her husband. In these letters, when writing of her many qualities, 'kind' was the word most often used.

This biography draws many of its sources and illustrations from the outstanding collections of Woolf manuscripts and possessions in the British Library, the Tate Gallery Archive and Chatto and Windus at Random House in London; the National Trust property that was once her home, Monk's House at Rodmell in Sussex; and the Berg Collection of the New York Public Library. Its purpose is not to present the many views of her expressed by critics, nor to assess the quality or value of her writing. Rather, it is intended to give a clear account of her life and works, to show who and what influenced her thought, and to introduce a writer whose works still have the power to touch the hearts and stimulate the minds of readers.

~ Acknowledgements

My greatest thanks go to Sally Brown, Senior Curator of Modern Literary Manuscripts at the British Library, whose support of my work on the manuscripts of Virginia Woolf has been invaluable. This book owes its existence to her. I should also like to thank the staffs of the Berg Collection, New York Public Library, the Tate Gallery Archive, the National Portrait Gallery Archive, the National Trust Photographic Library, Shortlands Library, and the Lilly Library, Indiana University. Finally, my thanks go to Anne Young, my editor at the British Library, for her unfailing good humour and support.

This book is dedicated to Rosemary Sumner, a great - and patient - teacher.

Ruth Webb   March 2000

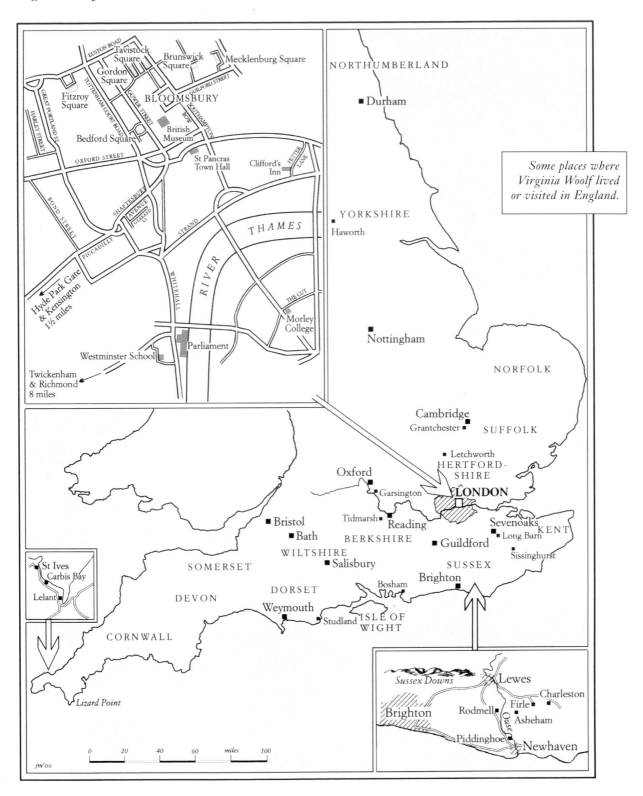

Some places where Virginia Woolf lived or visited in England.

〜 *Childhood*

Who was I then? Adeline Virginia Stephen, the second daughter of Leslie and Julia Prinsep Stephen, born on 25th January 1882, descended from a great many people, some famous, others obscure; born into a large connection, born not of rich parents, but of well-to-do parents, born into a very communicative, literate, letter writing, visiting, articulate, late nineteenth century world.

The 'large connection' to which Virginia Woolf refers in the above extract from her memoir, *A Sketch of the Past*, included her large and complex immediate family. Each of her parents had been married before and widowed. Her mother, Julia, came from an artistic family. Her first husband had been a barrister named Herbert Duckworth, and Julia had three Duckworth children when she married her second husband, Leslie Stephen. He had one daughter, Laura, from his first marriage. Together, Julia and Leslie Stephen had four more children. When the last was born in 1883, the children to whom Leslie Stephen was father or step-father were George Duckworth, aged 15; Stella Duckworth, aged 14; Gerald Duckworth, aged 13; Laura Stephen, aged 13; Vanessa Stephen, aged 4; Thoby Stephen, aged 3; Virginia Stephen, almost 2; and Adrian just born.

The Stephen family lived at 22 Hyde Park Gate, London. It was a large house on several floors, with basement and attic rooms, and was located just south of Kensington Gardens, one of the Royal Parks. The family employed servants, including those whose special duty it was to look after the children. Laura Stephen lived separately from the others. Her mother, Leslie's first wife, was a daughter of the writer William Thackeray. Her name was Minny, and she had been born in 1840. Immediately after Minny's birth, Thackeray's wife had become mentally unbalanced, and spent the rest of her life in nursing homes. During her lifetime, the term used for Mrs Thackeray's

The birthplace of Virginia Woolf, 22 Hyde Park Gate, today.

Author's photograph

condition was 'madness'. When Laura Stephen failed to develop as quickly as other children, Leslie worried that she had inherited her grandmother's madness, as well as the mental instability of some male members of his own family. Her behaviour and speech were unpredictable and she had limited powers of concentration. A woman was employed to look after her, as her personal nanny or 'nurse'. As the children of Julia and Leslie Stephen - Vanessa, Thoby, Virginia and Adrian - had a separate nursery, Laura was both part and not part of the household. When Virginia was five, Laura moved away from the family home to be cared for in the country.

It is as well that the subject of 'madness' in Leslie Stephen's family is mentioned early in a biographical account of his daughter. Many people who have never read Virginia Woolf's novels will know two things about her: that she was 'mad' and that she drowned herself. That her family and friends referred to her periods of mental instability as 'madness' and that she committed suicide at the age of 59 are both facts. But they are by no means the most interesting facts about her. Nevertheless, interest in them persists. A number of seemingly related elements are often noted regarding her 'madness': the odd, uncontrolled behaviour of her half-sister Laura; the mental illness of Laura's grandmother (no blood relation of Virginia's); the erratic behaviour, following a blow to the head, of one of Leslie Stephen's cousins; and the melancholy turn of Leslie's mind. These all pre-dated the life of Virginia, and the reader must decide to what extent heredity, childhood and adult experiences contributed to her periods of mental instability, and whether the proportionally greater part of her life and its achievements prove to be of more interest.

It was Vanessa, of all her siblings, to whom Virginia was closest throughout her life. She described their relationship as 'a close conspiracy'. When Virginia decided to kill herself, she wrote suicide notes to two people: to her husband, Leonard, and to Vanessa. In an interview recorded fifteen years after Virginia's death, Vanessa recalled that, when she and Virginia were small, Virginia asked her which of their parents Vanessa preferred. Vanessa, though greatly shocked by the

Virginia in 1884, held by her mother, Julia.

Random House, London

Virginia and her father, Leslie Stephen.

Random House, London

question, thought for a moment and then replied that, if she must make a choice, she would choose their mother. Virginia, however, 'on the whole, preferred my father,' said Vanessa. In the year that Virginia was born, Leslie Stephen took on the editorship of the new *Dictionary of National Biography*, generally referred to as the *DNB*. He spent ten years on this work, only in the last year being assisted by the man who succeeded him as editor. Highly respected as a scholar and writer, Virginia's father nevertheless agonized about his work on the *DNB* - as he did about much else - and was the dominant figure in the family.

Julia Stephen was considered very beautiful, although her children - perhaps Virginia more than Vanessa or their brothers - were not conscious of this. Somehow, for Virginia, Julia's beauty was inextricably linked with her motherhood. It was, Virginia wrote, a 'natural quality that a mother - she seemed typical, universal, yet our own in particular - had by virtue of being our mother'. And 'she was central', a fundamental element of childhood's happiness. As a late-Victorian woman of the upper-middle classes, Julia Stephen spent much of her time in helping those less fortunate than herself, and in writing letters. She was opposed to women's rights, including the right to vote in local or national government elections. Vanessa expressed the view that a lasting portrait of both their parents was to be found in Virginia's novel, *To the Lighthouse*, written long after their deaths.

Virginia was confident in the love of both her parents, but especially that of her father, for whom she was a favourite. Each summer from 1882 to 1894 the Stephen children spent two to three months by the sea in Cornwall. Leslie Stephen, on a walking tour there in 1881, had decided to take the lease on a large villa named Talland House. He described its position above the bay of St Ives as a 'pocket paradise'. Although the journey from London each summer was arduous, with children, servants and luggage, Julia agreed with her husband that the house, its garden and the proximity of the sea provided a delightful summer home for the children. A local resident remembered Leslie Stephen's enjoyment of playing in the sea with his children, and Virginia's memories of those summers seem bathed in a golden light:

Virginia, 'the demon bowler', playing wicket-keeper to her younger brother and batsman, Adrian, in the garden of Talland House, St Ives.

Tate Gallery Archive

It had, when we came there, a perfect view - right across the Bay to Godrevy Lighthouse. It had running down the hill, little lawns, surrounded by thick escallonia bushes, whose leaves one picked and pressed and smelt: it had so many corners and lawns that each was named: the coffee garden; the fountain; the cricket ground; the love corner…the strawberry bed; the kitchen garden; the pond; and the big tree.

A Sketch of the Past

The cricket ground mentioned above was the site of many of Virginia's sporting triumphs, and she was named by the family 'the demon bowler'. During her childhood, life in St Ives was 'ecstasy' - or so it seemed to her in her late fifties, when she wrote of the most important of all her memories:

hearing the waves breaking, one, two, one, two, and sending a splash of water over the beach; and then breaking, one, two, one, two, behind a yellow blind. It is of hearing the blind draw its little acorn across the floor as the wind blew

the blind out. It is of lying and hearing this plash and seeing this light, and
feeling, it is almost impossible that I should be here; of feeling the purest ecstasy
I can conceive.

A Sketch of the Past

Many guests stayed at Talland House, both family and friends. Amongst the latter was James Russell Lowell, the poet and essayist whom Leslie Stephen had met in America during the Civil War in 1863, and who later became the American ambassador in London. Although none of the children of Leslie and Julia were baptised, they had the secular equivalents of godparents and Virginia's was Lowell. Another expatriate American friend of their father's, the novelist Henry James, features in the family photograph albums.

The front page of an early edition of Hyde Park Gate News, *produced by the Stephen children.*

British Library, Additional MS 70725, folio 13

Both in St Ives and at home in London, from 1891 to 1895, the children produced weekly issues of the family journal, the *Hyde Park Gate News*. Vanessa recalled, when interviewed, that Virginia watched and waited in excitement to hear her parents' opinion of it. Her mother's verdict on one edition, as she handed it to her husband, was that it was 'rather clever, I think'. The cleverness often resided in the children's use of irony and humour at each other's expense - and at the expense of their parents and other adults. Two serial stories ran through several editions; even at this early stage in Virginia's writing career, she was not content with short pieces of journalism alone. And Leslie Stephen considered that, even as a child, Virginia showed sufficient talent to 'be an author in time'.

A Series of Blows

Virginia's childhood in the 1880s and 1890s had not only its joys, but also its miseries and disappointments. Nevertheless, as a member of a large and relatively prosperous family, she was essentially happy and secure until the first great tragedy of her life. It occurred when she was 13 years old. In the *Hyde Park Gate News* of 4 March 1895 there appears a report that for two weeks 'Mrs Leslie Stephen has been in bed with the influenza'. Although Julia apparently recovered, within less than two months she became dangerously ill with rheumatic fever. The Duckworth children, by then in their mid-to late twenties, decided to return home from their European holiday in the last week of April. Stella was particularly concerned to be with her mother. But Julia lived only a week or so longer, dying on 5 May 1895, aged forty-nine.

In the face of death, Virginia was disturbed to observe that she - like Septimus Warren Smith in *Mrs Dalloway*, a character she was to create almost thirty years later - felt 'nothing whatever'. She was unsettled by her reactions; for example, when she kissed the face of her dead mother, she recoiled at its coldness - 'it was like kissing cold iron'. It was these physical responses rather than her emotional condition that she wrote of in later life. It is clear from her family's comments at the time that she was deeply distressed by the loss of her mother, and suffered a prolonged period of emotional disturbance, usually referred to as her first 'breakdown'. Although, near the end of her life, Virginia Woolf wrote in *A Sketch of the Past* about her feelings following her mother's death, she wrote nothing at the time that it happened. Her father's letters and her half-sister Stella's diary entries suggest that it took more than a year for her deeply unsettled condition to pass.

In addition to concerning herself with Virginia's ill-health, and dealing with her own grief, Stella Duckworth found that she had also to bear the brunt of her stepfather's mourning. Leslie felt in despair that he had not loved Julia as he ought, and endlessly sought Stella's reassurance that he had not been a bad husband to her mother. Other emotional demands were being made of Stella at this time which were more pleasing than those of her stepfather. During her mother's lifetime, Stella had refused Jack Hills as a possible husband but in the summer of 1896 she accepted his proposal of marriage. When they returned from their honeymoon, they took up residence at number 24 Hyde Park Gate.

But Stella's fate was not to be happy. She returned from her honeymoon unwell, experiencing abdominal pain which continued for three months. The diagnoses altered during that time. She was pregnant, but she also had peritonitis. Although the latter was diagnosed early, Stella was not operated upon until it was too late. She died in July 1897, when Virginia was 15 years old. During the days immediately before her death, Stella had spent time with Virginia, who was not altogether well. Virginia had a high temperature, and so stayed in Stella's home and was nursed by her. A combination of an excited state of 'nervousness', feelings of rebelliousness against Stella - who was to some extent taking her mother's rôle - and irritation at visitors who seemed interested only in Stella, created in Virginia strong feelings of resentment. And so, when Stella died suddenly, Virginia felt once more a tremendous sense of loss, this time combined with feelings of guilt and bewilderment at this '*second* blow of death'.

Vanessa, at 18, was now the 'woman' of the family, making the household arrangements and enduring Leslie's weekly inspection of the household accounts. But in addition to her domestic duties, she pursued her vocation as an artist. Each day she left the house for her art classes, whilst Virginia stayed at home, writing the diary she had begun that year, diligently reading the books her father had recommended, and studying Greek and Latin. Her reading included essays and prose from the Elizabethan period to her own day and masses of

Victorian fiction. She took classes in history, Greek and Latin with Dr George Warr - an eminent translator of the classics who was a founder of the Ladies' Department of King's College, now part of the University of London – and Clara Pater, the sister of the essayist and critic Walter Pater.

During these years, when Virginia received a little formal education outside the home, her brothers were taking the traditional educational routes open to boys from upper-middle-class families such as theirs. In 1894, the year before his mother's death, Thoby had become a boarder at Clifton College in Bristol, and in 1896, the year before Stella died, Adrian had entered Westminster School, continuing to live at home in London. He came home each day with tales of his school. Thoby, as an older brother away at boarding school, was a more distant figure. Virginia's studies were less structured than, and in her opinion inferior to, those of her brothers - social and family life were thought to be more important for girls than intellectual achievement.

In the summer of 1898, their cousin William Wyamar Vaughan married Madge Symonds, a published writer who had spent the winter of 1889 with the Stephen family at Hyde Park Gate. At the time of her marriage, she was, to the teenage Virginia, an immensely attractive figure. In adulthood, Virginia recalled 'this was the woman I adored! I see myself now standing in the night nursery at Hyde Park Gate, washing my hands, & saying to myself "At this moment she is actually under this roof".' By contrast to the vibrant Madge, Miss Pater, Virginia's classics tutor, was 'pathetic' and 'desolate'. She taught Virginia for just over a year before she was superseded by a woman who was to have a tremendous impact upon Virginia's intellectual life - Janet Case. She introduced an element of rigour into Virginia's studies that she perceived had been lacking under her previous tutors.

In 1899, Thoby had entered Trinity College, Cambridge where, in 1900 he invited his sisters to attend the May Week celebrations. They returned the following year, and it was at tea, chaperoned by their Aunt Kate - who was the principal of Newnham, a women's college - that Thoby's friends Clive Bell and Leonard Woolf met Vanessa and Virginia, the women they would later marry.

During the years when the Trinity College visits took place, Virginia's half-brother George Duckworth determined that Vanessa should move in very different circles from those to be found in the Cambridge of Thoby and his friends. George had inherited a private income and readily spent money on Vanessa, buying her jewellery and an Arab mare to ride each morning. But George's wishes and Vanessa's were very different. When Vanessa finally refused to pretend to enjoy the social gatherings so important to George, and her obstinacy became a real impediment, he transferred his attentions to her younger sister, Virginia. It was she who now received gifts of jewellery, but she, too, was socially awkward - not, like her sister, through boredom, but through shyness. She talked either too little or too much, and generally made things very awkward for George. It was in her memoir, *Hyde Park Gate*, written in the early 1920s that Virginia Woolf revealed the full extent of her suffering. The social humiliation had been bad enough.

The 15 year-old Virginia sitting with the 28 year-old George Duckworth, who is clasping her hand, 1897.

Tate Gallery Archive

At last – at last – the evening was over.

I went up to my room, took off my beautiful white satin dress, and unfastened the three pink carnations which had been pinned to my breast…Many different things were whirling round in my mind…Ah, how pleasant it would be to stretch out in bed, fall asleep and forget them all! Sleep had almost come to me. The room was dark. The house silent. Then, creaking stealthily, the door opened; treading gingerly, someone entered. "Who?" I cried. "Don't be frightened," George whispered. "And don't turn on the light, oh beloved. Beloved–" and he flung himself on my bed, and took me in his arms.

Hyde Park Gate

This account of George's disturbing conduct was given, over twenty years after it had occurred, to the group of Virginia's close family and friends who would gather as members of what they called the Memoir Club. Virginia recorded in her diary that E.M. Forster, the novelist and one of those close friends who was present when she read her account, praised it as the 'best thing you ever did'. She found his

Janet Case, Virginia and Vanessa in Firle Park, 1911.

Random House, London

praise disconcerting; if a writer whom she admired thought this writing her best, 'I'm a mere scribbler', she wrote.

Another memoir, *Old Bloomsbury*, written within a year of *Hyde Park Gate*, suggests that George had treated her in this way on other occasions: 'There would be a tap at the door; the light would be turned out and George would fling himself on my bed, cuddling and kissing and otherwise embracing me.' Vanessa confirmed Virginia's claims concerning what she called 'George's malefactions' near the time of their happening. Janet Case was also unsettled by George's fondling of his half-sister on the occasions when he came into the room where Janet taught Greek to Virginia.

During these years, Leslie Stephen's hearing deteriorated and his irascibility increased. Vanessa, as the eldest daughter, endured Leslie's hectoring over household management and much else, and all the family experienced embarrassment over one outcome of their father's ill-temper and deafness combined. He took to groaning loudly over what he perceived to be the miseries of his life, or when visitors had outstayed their welcome. Stories of his embarrassing outburts were doubtless told long after his death, for a grandson whom he never knew, writing the first official biography of Virginia Woolf, wrote:

> *Leslie's teatime groans were, only too often, the prelude to something far worse. Leslie was deaf enough not to hear, or to pretend not to hear, his own conversations with himself.*
>
> *'Why won't that young man go?' he would suddenly demand in a dreadfully audible voice. Or again, when his old friend Frederick Waymouth Gibbs had, for a space of twenty minutes or so, imparted a great mass of information concerning the Dominion of Canada, Leslie would produce an enormous groan and remark, in a deafening whisper: 'Oh Gibbs, what a bore you are.'*

At this time, with their father a morose figure, their mother and motherly half-sister dead, their brothers absorbed in their own triumphs and miseries, and their half-brothers equally absorbed in their interests, the Stephen sisters experienced little love or affection other than that which they gave to each other. In the summer of 1900, George expressed his concern to Virginia that Vanessa and Stella's widower, Jack Hills, were spending too much time together. He was not alone in thinking this relationship scandalous; his view was supported by their maternal aunt, Mary Fisher, and by the laws of England. Until 1907, marriage between a widower and his sister-in-law was illegal. Flummoxed by the news, Virginia found herself in the position of being expected to castigate her favourite sister on behalf of her least favourite brother. On speaking to Vanessa and finding herself accused - 'So you take their side too' - Virginia realized that she was not on 'their side' at all. Then, as always, her strongest allegiance was to her sister. Their father, too, took Vanessa's side. Despite his domineering qualities, he was concerned that his daughters were independent thinkers who could make their own way in the world. When recalling the incident, near the end of her life, Virginia recorded what she called 'father's sense'. Ultimately, however, the relationship did not last and George was relieved that the family had avoided a public scandal.

The 'six feet high' Violet Dickinson with Virginia.

Tate Gallery Archive

Public acclaim and reflected glory were instead to come the following year. In 1901, Leslie Stephen was awarded an Honorary D.Litt from the University of Oxford, and in 1902, persuaded by his children, he accepted the King's honour of the KCB, thus becoming Sir Leslie Stephen. The year of 1902 was also important to Virginia, in that another relationship began to flourish: Violet Dickinson became her closest friend.

Virginia was 20 and Violet was 37. Violet had known the family for many years, having been a friend of Stella. She had only one 'fault' in the opinion of Sir Leslie: 'she is six feet high'. In Virginia's opinion, she was full of 'youthful zeal' despite her 37 years, 'always talking & laughing & entering into whatever was going on'. The whole family liked her and she proved to be a valuable and loving friend to Virginia for many years. During her lifetime, Virginia wrote Violet over three hundred letters, most of them in the five years following the summer of 1902. Virginia would ask for Violet's opinion of her writing, recognizing that 'literary advice is a very ticklish thing'. She also grew to depend upon Violet for emotional support, for Sir Leslie's health had deteriorated earlier in the year that she and Violet had become close friends and it was to deteriorate further.

In the autumn of 1902, Adrian left the family home and joined his brother Thoby at Trinity College, Cambridge. Shortly before Christmas the same year, Sir Leslie was operated upon. He had cancer of the bowel and knew he had not long to live. He grew more melancholy and, with both Thoby and Adrian in Cambridge, made even more demands upon his daughters, especially Vanessa. George and Gerald Duckworth, instead of providing support, simply irritated their half-sisters. It became increasingly obvious that, once Sir Leslie had died, the Stephens and the Duckworths would have to part.

But he did not die as quickly as had been predicted. There was another summer holiday shared with Violet and other friends in 1903, and a resumption of Greek lessons with Janet Case in the autumn. Nevertheless, it was clear that Sir Leslie was dying and, apart from dealing with their own feelings, Virginia and Vanessa had to cope

Leslie Stephen in academic cap and gown.

Tate Gallery Archive

with the constant stream of visitors to their ailing father. Virginia, like Vanessa, had negative feelings for her father but she remained deeply fond of him and, when he finally died in February 1904, she felt 'I never helped him as I might have done'. In the same month, the Stephens and the Duckworths left London for the country, and in April all but George went to Venice.

Virginia had been unsettled by the aftermath of her father's death and, for a time in Italy, was distracted and delighted. The Stephens travelled on to Florence, where Violet joined them. Adrian returned to Cambridge, and Thoby left on a walking tour later that month, leaving Virginia, Vanessa and Violet to continue travelling around Italy before returning to London via Paris.

It was early in May by the time they arrived at Hyde Park Gate. Returning to the house in which her father had so recently died, Virginia experienced no comforting sense of homecoming. In Paris, their time had been spent talking about the visual arts, visiting Rodin's studio, living in a world that satisfied Vanessa's needs. Vanessa had felt an enormous sense of release at her father's death and now, finally, she was free to pursue her vocation. Virginia felt quite differently. She longed to be a writer - her father's profession. She felt guilty and miserably isolated. The travel had jangled her nerves, and the guilt and the grief made them worse. Being back in a house so redolent with memories of the dead - her mother, her half-sister and now her father - proved too much for Virginia. She began to experience headaches and hear voices, she spoke incoherently, and soon she lost touch with the reality of those around her.

During her illness, even her bond with Vanessa was broken. Sir George Savage, who had been a friend of their father and was a specialist in mental disorders, took charge of her treatment. She refused to eat and had to be cared for by three nurses, all of whom she hated. Eventually, Violet was permitted to take Virginia to Hertfordshire, where Violet shared a house with her brother. There Virginia's delusions continued: she heard the birds outside her window singing in Greek; the King, too, was outside the window - amongst the azaleas, not singing but using foul language. Eventually, she made a feeble attempt at suicide by throwing herself from the window but it was not high enough for her to do herself any real harm. By September she had recovered sufficiently to be allowed to join her family on holiday in Nottingham. In October, she went to stay with her father's only sister in Cambridge, where Adrian was still studying.

Here began her real recovery, through writing. One of her cousins had married a historian, F.W. Maitland, who had known Leslie in the St Ives days. He was writing a biography of Sir Leslie, and asked Virginia to read her parents' letters to one another. He also asked her to write a brief description of her father's relationship with his children, which was published as part of the biography. It was as well that she had this occupation, as her aunt was irritating her and she was anxious to return to London.

In her absence from home, great changes had taken place. The Stephens and the Duckworths had parted; the Stephens now lived in Bloomsbury.

Bloomsbury Groups

Fitzroy Square on a winter day.

Unknown photographer

At the turn of the century, Bloomsbury - the location of the British Museum - was not considered a good neighbourhood by the upper-middle class. The children of Sir Leslie Stephen, born into this class and accustomed to the established elegance of Kensington, would not have been expected to live in such a place. Characteristic of the area, however, are garden squares surrounded by tall terraced houses which, in their enclosed form, echo the colleges of Oxford and Cambridge. It was to Bloomsbury that many of Thoby's Cambridge friends came to live, to meet together, and to get to know the Stephen sisters whom they had first met at Cambridge. In the summer of 1904, Vanessa had found a house at 46 Gordon Square in Bloomsbury, and in November Virginia finally left Cambridge and began to live and write there.

Virginia's struggle to become a writer was made more difficult by prevailing beliefs about the treatment of mental disorder. In lay terms, Virginia suffered periodically from a type of manic-depressive illness. This had both physical and psychological elements: her pulse would race, her temperature would fluctuate, and her ability to eat and sleep would be affected; to others and to herself she would talk incoherently and incessantly, and she heard voices no one else could hear. The treatment for such symptoms varied somewhat from doctor to doctor, but generally the patient was prescribed complete rest. This meant that reading and writing, believed to excite the patient dangerously, were forbidden. For Virginia, such prohibitions were a torture. At 46 Gordon Square she was at last free to write.

It was through Violet Dickinson that Virginia was able to place her first article, in *The Guardian*, a weekly newspaper for the clergy. The Women's Supplement was edited by Margaret Lyttelton, a friend of Violet's. The article was about the home of the Brontë sisters in Haworth, which Virginia had visited earlier in the year. It was published in December 1904, and she had at last managed to get her foot in the door of the house of letters. In January 1905, declared well again by Dr Savage, Virginia could read and write at liberty in her room at the top of the tall house. The sense of freedom emboldened Virginia to accept an offer of teaching, unpaid, at Morley College. The college had been founded, beneath the stage of the Old Vic Theatre, as a place of learning for working-class men and women to attend after a day's work. The first class she was asked to teach began at 9 o'clock in the evening. She taught sessions on English literature and history, and made use of her travels in Italy. The classes were very small - initially of two women, then of four - and later in the year included both men and women. Virginia found the experience of teaching unsatisfactory. The work did not pay, took an inordinate amount of time to prepare - Virginia was always meticulous in her work, be it reading, writing or teaching - and gave little or no pleasure. However, she struggled on for almost three years, to the end of 1907, before giving it up. Although she left the work more than willingly, it made a lasting impression upon her - she had come into regular contact with working-class men and women, an experience she was to make use of when writing her novels.

A rare picture of Duncan Grant, a cousin of Lytton Strachey, Thoby and Virginia Stephen dressed formally; photograph taken in The Post Card Studio on the Strand in London - undated

British Library Additional MS 58120, folio 133 verso

Shortly after Virginia began teaching, Thoby initiated what was to become an institution for the Stephens and their friends: a weekly evening gathering. The practice amongst their parents' generation, of declaring oneself 'at home' for visitors once a week was transformed into a far more informal gathering by the Stephens. They called these meetings simply 'Thursday Evenings' and, rather than wearing formal clothes, they wore whatever they felt comfortable in, and talked about things that they felt mattered. Initially, Virginia remained silent at these gatherings but she was subsequently awed by the brilliance of Thoby's friends' reasoning, and ultimately drawn into their circle. This was the beginning of what has become known as The Bloomsbury Group.

The term 'Group' suggests a specific group of people who self-consciously distinguished themselves from and excluded others. This was in no strict sense true. In later years, those who had been amongst the first to attend the Thursday Evenings would refer to Old Bloomsbury, to signify the small group of Thoby's friends who came to talk or sit silently at 46 Gordon Square. These early visitors included men Thoby had known at Cambridge: Clive Bell, who later became an art critic; Walter Lamb, Secretary of the Royal Academy; Desmond MacCarthy, a literary journalist; Lytton Strachey, a biographer and essayist; Saxon Sydney-Turner, a civil servant; and Edward Hilton Young, a politician. Leonard Woolf had visited Gordon Square shortly after the Stephens had moved there, but before the Thursday Evenings were instituted. He was unable to be part of that initial group as, immediately after visiting the Stephens, he took up a post in the Colonial Service, part of the British Administration in Ceylon. Virginia was not to see him for seven years.

Virginia continued to experiment with writing. She produced reviews for *The Guardian* and now also *The Times Literary Supplement*, for which her father had written. Journalism provided her with a small income, and she began unpaid work on fiction. During her lifetime, most of this early work was not published. Fifty and more years after her death, almost everything she wrote has been made available to the reading public, through paperback editions, scholarly tomes and graduate theses. But in 1905, all that she had had published was her journalism. Although some of her articles were rejected, she continued to write and rewrite, always wanting to improve her prose. She prepared her Morley College classes equally carefully. Nevertheless, she had a considerable amount of time for reading, translating the classics, and writing descriptive, imaginative, even fantastical works. She was twenty-three and wanted to make her mark on the world; but she also wrote simply for her own pleasure.

In the early spring of 1905, Virginia travelled to Spain and Portugal with Adrian, who was in his final undergraduate year at Cambridge. She recorded all she

saw in a journal, which was to prove of practical use when she returned to London and received a request for a review of books about Spain. As spring dissolved into summer, Virginia spent time in Oxford, Cambridge, Sussex and Berkshire. During this time, Clive Bell began to spend more time with Vanessa, and proposed to her for the first time. He was refused but not in a manner that made him feel that he might not be successful on a later occasion.

Since the summer before the death of their mother in 1895, the Stephen children had not revisited Cornwall. Ten years after her death, Julia's four Stephen children travelled in August to Carbis Bay, about a mile along the coast from St Ives. They stayed there almost as long as they had when they were children, inviting friends, and even Gerald Duckworth, to stay. The place had inevitably changed in their years of absence, but local people remembered them as children and spoke affectionately of their parents, especially their mother. On the evening of their arrival they walked up to Talland House and 'hung there like ghosts'. In one sense, the journey served as a laying of ghosts. Nostalgia had drawn them back to St Ives, and they enjoyed the end of the summer there once more; but an adult life in London awaited them, and they returned to Gordon Square early in October.

Talland House today. The roof extension (top windows) was added after the Stephens had given up leasing the house each summer

William Heller, Digital Imagemakers, St Ives

Once they were back in London, Vanessa set about establishing the Friday Club for discussing the fine arts. Virginia occasionally joined her sister, Clive Bell, Henry Lamb (brother of Walter, a Thursday Evening visitor), Pernel Strachey (one of Lytton's elder sisters), Saxon Sydney-Turner and others, but took little part in the proceedings of the club. Her brothers were both studying law and, although Virginia had managed to persuade both of them, as well as Clive Bell and Vanessa, to help her by teaching drawing, Greek and Latin to her Morley College students earlier in the year, they soon lost interest. Each of the brothers and sisters, therefore, pursued their careers, Virginia and Vanessa both making some money at this early stage.

The sisters visited Yorkshire the following spring, staying near Madge and Will Vaughan and, in the summer, Virginia once again visited her Cambridge aunt and Violet Dickinson in Hertfordshire. The four siblings spent a brief time in Norfolk together in August before the brothers left for Italy, arranging to meet Virginia and Vanessa in Greece in September. The trip was ultimately to prove disastrous. Fortunately, Violet Dickinson accompanied the sisters and, when Vanessa became ill with appendicitis, Violet took care of her. Virginia and her brothers continued to travel together in Greece and Turkey well into October, Virginia finding that her knowledge of ancient Greek was of no help in communicating with twentieth-century Athenians. Thoby returned home before the others, who finally arrived in London at the beginning of November.

Violet was now ailing with what was to be diagnosed as typhoid and, when they reached home, they found Thoby also suffering from the disease, although it was not accurately diagnosed for another ten days. Virginia and Adrian's health remained good, and they ministered to their brother and sister, Virginia also writing daily to Violet, who was still unwell. Clive visited regularly, and Vanessa's condition improved, but Thoby's did not. A complication of typhoid was peritonitis, which had killed Stella. To prevent this danger, the doctors operated on Thoby, knowing that

Madge Vaughan and her children, Barbara, Janet, David and Halford. Janet would become Dame Janet Vaughan, an eminent doctor and principal of Somerville College Oxford, whose research Virginia would make use of in A Room of One's Own.

Random House, London

the operation itself was dangerous. The fever worsened and, three days after the operation, Thoby died.

Virginia, whilst grieving for her brother and caring for her sister, was advised not to inform Violet - who was slowly recovering from typhoid - of Thoby's death. Thus she found herself writing to Violet on the day of Thoby's death that they were 'going on well'; and, still, three days after his funeral she was writing 'Thoby is going on splendidly'. She kept this up for nearly a month before Violet discovered the truth and Virginia was forced to explain the reasons for her deception. Thoby's friend, Lytton Strachey, visited immediately on receiving the news. Clive Bell also came. Two days after Thoby's death he proposed once more to Vanessa and was this time accepted. Although she understood Vanessa's happiness, Virginia experienced the engagement of her sister, at this distressing time, as a second loss.

Adrian was closest to Virginia in age and, having attended a London school before university, he had spent time with her every day, but he and Virginia had never been emotionally very close. Lytton Strachey understood this well and wrote to Leonard Woolf of Thoby's death, adding, 'Poor Virginia! And Adrian! They must set up house together now. The mind recoils.' Virginia felt the loss of her elder brother she was to continue to feel it for twenty or more years - and Adrian was no substitute. She expressed sympathy for his loss of a brother, but of her siblings, Adrian would have been her last choice as a companion.

Nevertheless, it was clear that brother and sister should leave 46 Gordon Square to Vanessa and Clive, after their honeymoon the following spring. It was Virginia who found a house nearby in Fitzroy Square. She felt that her sister had been taken away from her, and at the same time she wished to assert her own independence. Her feelings for Clive, who had been a friend of her dead brother and was now married to her sister, were complex and unsettling. Clive and Virginia had frequent disagreements, but she valued his comments on her writing. She was delighted with her personal domain on the second floor at 29 Fitzroy Square, having double windows installed to keep out traffic noise, and decorating it in bright red and green.

That autumn, Virginia, who had written a number of pieces of short fiction, began to write what was to become her first published novel. She was teaching still, although she was soon to give it up, and continued her own education with reading.

She and Adrian led an informal life, but were still supported by servants who took care of all domestic arrangements.

Brother and sister reinstated the Thursday Evenings, and at 46 Gordon Square, the Play Reading Society was established. At the first meeting, the Bells and Stephens were joined by Lytton Strachey and Saxon Sydney-Turner. In addition to these gatherings, Virginia and Adrian visited the theatre and musical events. They were often out of the house enjoying themselves in and around London. Virginia had regularly to sit for her portrait, and began to establish an independent life for herself now that her sister was pregnant and would soon have even less time for sisterly companionship. She permitted herself a flirtation with Walter Headlam, a Cambridge academic many years her senior, who asked if he might dedicate his translation of the *Agamemnon* to her. Although flattered by his attachment to her, Virginia did not treat his attentions seriously and, when he died, aged 42, in the summer of 1908, the loss did not affect her greatly.

Vanessa's first son, Julian, was born in February 1908. Although marriage and motherhood inevitably separated Virginia and Vanessa, they nevertheless spent a great deal of time together, both in London and on numerous holidays that year. There was another return to St Ives, where Adrian and Virginia were joined by the Bells, and after visits closer to home in July, Virginia met Vanessa and Clive in Bath and travelled to Italy with them in the later summer months. In the autumn there were more play readings, at which they were joined by Lytton Strachey who also accompanied Virginia and Adrian on a late autumn holiday to the Lizard in Cornwall. Lytton could be both an exciting and an intimidating presence. He had come to Gordon Square as soon as he had heard of Thoby's death, and had been a

Above:

Portrait in chalk of Virginia, by Francis Dodd, 1908.

National Portrait Gallery, London

Opposite:

A rare picture of Lytton Strachey laughing, at Asheham.

Tate Gallery Archive

loyal, amusing and stimulating friend to Thoby's remaining family. He and Clive had been at Cambridge together and had taken part in creating 'Old Bloomsbury'. In the atmosphere of total freedom of speech that prevailed amongst these old companions, it was not surprising that it was Lytton who broke the final taboo. One evening the sisters were sitting together waiting for Clive to return home when suddenly

> *the door opened and the long and sinister figure of Mr. Lytton Strachey stood*
> *on the threshold. He pointed his finger at a stain on Vanessa's white dress.*
> *'Semen?' he said.*
> *Can one really say it? I thought & we burst out laughing. With that one word*
> *all barriers of reticence and reserve went down.*

Virginia's literary work in 1908 extended to writing articles for *The Cornhill* magazine, which her father had edited before beginning work on the *DNB*. She continued to write what she then called 'Melymbrosia', eventually published in 1915 as her first novel, *The Voyage Out*. In 1909 she asked her brother-in-law, Clive, to give her his opinion of the chapters she had written. Virginia's relationship with Clive had altered since his marriage to her sister. She had initially thought him inadequate and unsuitable, and during the first year of their marriage had got into frequent disagreements with him. Once Julian was born, especially when the Bells and Stephens were on holiday, Clive sought escape from his son's crying and Vanessa's absorption in her child. Virginia, too, felt no desire to stay indoors, and she would join Clive in long walks. An intimacy grew up between them; there was no sexual contact, but the relationship was sufficiently serious to give pain to Vanessa. Clive had had lovers before he married Vanessa, who knew his nature. She also knew her sister's, and saw that there was no real commitment or passion on Virginia's part. As with Walter Headlam, Virginia was only flirting, but this time it was with her own brother-in-law. A number of letters were exchanged, in many of which Clive commented on her novel in progress. Her letters to him reveal a willingness to benefit from his criticisms.

During this time, Virginia was becoming, in the chaste manner characteristic of her, more intimate with Lytton Strachey. He was frank about sexual matters, was

openly homosexual, and he and Virginia enjoyed each other's company. Their closest friends began to speculate on the possibility of their marrying. Virginia, in one of her letters to Clive, declared, 'I am not in love with him, nor is there any sign that he is in love with me.' In spite of this declaration at Christmas 1908, in February 1909 Lytton, two weeks before his twenty-ninth birthday, proposed to Virginia, now aged twenty-seven. She accepted him. Only Lytton's account survives:

I proposed to Virginia, and was accepted. It was an awkward moment, as you may imagine, especially as I realized, the very minute it was happening, that the whole thing was repulsive to me. Her sense was amazing, and luckily it turned out that she's not in love. The result was that I was able to manage a fairly honourable retreat. The whole story is really rather amusing and singular.

A sketch in a letter from Dora Carrington to Lytton Strachey of Virginia and Lytton ice-skating.

British Library Additional MS 62897, folio 173 verso

They agreed, within twenty-four hours of the proposal, that they had both been foolish to contemplate marriage, and each was relieved to be released by the other. They remained friends all their lives and Clive Bell remembered that Lytton, when Clive had been visiting him in the country during the First World War, had asked, 'Lovers apart, whom would you most like to see coming up the drive?' When Clive had paused to consider the question, Lytton had supplied the answer, 'Virginia, of course.'

Later in the month of the proposal, Virginia went to visit her aunt, Caroline Emelia Stephen, in Cambridge. It was to be her last visit, for her aunt was to die early in April, 1909. More significantly for Virginia, her aunt was to leave her a legacy of £2,500, providing her with an income for life. Shortly after receiving news of the legacy, Virginia left for Florence with Vanessa and Clive. She did not enjoy the holiday, although the group of expatriate literary people she encountered provided her with models for some of the characters in her early novels. She was not in a calm frame of mind and the tensions between Virginia,

Vanessa and Clive caused her to return to London alone. She was in London only briefly before travelling to Cambridge and experiencing another emotionally unsettling event. Edward Hilton Young, who had been one of the early visitors to Thoby's Thursday Evenings, took her out in a punt and proposed to her. She gave no definite response and remained uncertain how to respond for some months. In August, she wrote to Vanessa, 'I gather you don't think much of Hilton Young…the truth is I don't think he will do; and whenever we meet we feel the incongruity'.

This same summer a new woman friend came into her life. Lady Ottoline Morrell had moved to Bloomsbury in 1906 when her husband had become a Member of Parliament. She had met Vanessa and Clive earlier in the year and attended a Thursday Evening at 29 Fitzroy Square. Ottoline's appearance was striking, and her love-life was as colourful as her clothes. She was nine years older than Virginia, and only slowly became her friend. Initially, and for many years, they were ambivalent about one another, but over more than thirty years, coming into regular contact in each other's homes, they grew fonder of each other. As Virginia's nephew and first biographer wrote, Ottoline 'brought petticoats, frivolity and champagne to the buns, the buggery and the high thinking of Fitzroy Square'. On Ottoline's death, in 1938, Virginia wrote an obituary for *The Times*:

Lady Ottoline Morrell with her daughter, Julian.

National Portrait Gallery, London

The great lady who suddenly appeared in the world of artists and writers immediately before the War easily lent herself to caricature. It was impossible not to exclaim in amazement at the strangeness; at the pearls, at the brocades, at the idealisms and exaltations. Again, with what imperious directness, like that of an artist intolerant of the conventional and the humdrum, she singled out the people she admired for qualities that she was often the first to detect and champion, and brought together at Bedford Square and then at Garsington, Prime Ministers and painters, Bishops and freethinkers, the famous and the obscure!…The 'great hostess' was very humble in the presence of those who could create beauty; and very generous; and very sincere.

It seems fitting that, having met so Wagnerian a character as Ottoline, Virginia was to travel to the Wagner Festival at Bayreuth in August 1909. With Adrian and Saxon, who had a great love of Wagner's music, she travelled for almost a month through Germany, and expanded her knowledge of the country and its music. On her return to England, she immediately made preparations to spend time with Vanessa and her family, initially in Salisbury, then in Studland in Dorset. They were joined there by one of their early Thursday Evenings friends, Walter Lamb, who began to be drawn to Virginia. His feelings were not reciprocated, but he did not lose hope - alas.

Virginia's hopes that the *Cornhill Magazine* would provide regular work were dashed at this point, through the editor's rejection of an imaginative piece she had presented as a review. Within two or three weeks of the rejection, she was travelling again, this time to stay in Cambridge for a few days. She also decided, on the spur of the moment, to spend Christmas without any of the family, in Lelant, Cornwall. The following March she was to return here with Vanessa, Clive and the baby Julian, who was beginning to interest her.

Between the two visits, Virginia was involved to a limited degree in the Votes for Women campaign and, much more spectacularly, in what is now referred to as the 'Dreadnought Hoax'. Astonishing though it may now seem, Adrian and a Cambridge friend of his, Horace de Vere Cole, convincingly presented themselves to the Royal Navy as officials from the Foreign Office who wished to escort Abyssinian visitors around the Dreadnought, a new warship. Masquerading as the Emperor of Abyssinia and his train, Virginia, Duncan Grant - a cousin of Lytton's and two other friends applied body make-up and false facial hair, and dressed themselves in turbans and long, colourful robes. They were met at Weymouth by a naval band, a red carpet and a guard of honour. Part of the pleasure for Adrian in

The report of the Dreadnought Hoax in the Daily Mirror. *Those involved are, from left to right, Virginia, Guy Ridley, Adrian, Anthony Buxton, Duncan Grant and Horace de Vere Cole.*

British Library, Newspaper Library.

mounting the hoax came from the knowledge that a maternal cousin, Commander William Fisher, would escort the party around the ship. Both falsely bearded, Virginia and Adrian shook hands with him. Adrian, the 'official interpreter', soon forgot the little Swahili he had learned and spoke in half-remembered lines from Virgil's *Æneid* to his sister and friends. Virginia and Duncan spoke gibberish. Fearful of being found out, and feeling sheepish about the courtesy with which they had been received, once having seen the ship they left in a hurry, catching a train back to London. The majority of the hoaxers wished to remain silent about the affair, but Horace de Vere Cole wanted publicity, and informed both the press and the Foreign Office. As a consequence, two newspapers, the *Daily Mirror* and *Daily Express*, covered the story, causing much embarrassment; questions were asked in Parliament. If the young Stephens had wanted to scandalize their stuffy relations, they had certainly scored a success.

The fuss continued for some time, during which the Stephens and Bells attempted to continue with their accustomed way of life. A new friend, the painter and art critic Roger Fry, gave a talk to the Friday Club. The Bells' association with him was to grow as the year progressed towards an exhibition that he mounted to run from November 1910 to January 1911, 'Manet and the Post-Impressionists'. A week or so after his talk, Virginia decided to join Vanessa and Clive in the part of Cornwall she had visited the previous Christmas. The excitement of the Dreadnought hoax, the unwanted public attention of its aftermath, and the difficult and troubling relationships with her sister and brother-in-law all combined to upset Virginia's fragile equilibrium. When she returned to London the following week, she realized she must take to her bed and Dr Savage was called. His perennial prescription of complete rest was translated into a three-week stay in Studland with Vanessa (pregnant again) and her family. From this 'rest-cure', Virginia returned to London, only to experience more severe headaches, aversion to food and all the old symptoms. Adrian and Clive took her on a couple of outings but by June she needed to be taken away by the Bells for another rest-cure. Vanessa, after two weeks, realized that professional help was needed. She herself was almost eight months pregnant and felt that she would soon be incapable of caring for her sister. She returned to London to see Dr Savage and it was decided that Virginia should go to a nursing home to take a month's rest.

Virginia and Clive Bell at Studland Bay in 1910.

Miss Thomas, to whose nursing home in Twickenham Virginia was sent, was charmed by Virginia who, despite being ill, brightened Miss Thomas's life and made her feel 'of consequence to herself' for the first time. The resulting affection between them was a help to Virginia in later years. The necessary quiet of life in Twickenham nevertheless bored Virginia and she took advantage of Miss Thomas's devotion, continually breaking the rules of the house regarding rest, dress and food. She persuaded Miss Thomas to accompany her to Cornwall, and finally managed to return to London in September. Her second nephew, Quentin, was a few weeks old and within another week Virginia and the Bells were back at Studland.

〜 *New Friends*

After her stay in Studland, Virginia felt she was well again, and was ready to return to London in October. Within a month of her return in November 1910, Virginia was engaged in the Votes for Women campaign, and the Post-Impressionist exhibition organized by Roger Fry was causing a stir. Dr Savage, Miss Thomas and Vanessa believed the excitement of London life was the very thing that Virginia should try to avoid or, at least, ration. Time spent in the country had had evident therapeutic effects, and Virginia was persuaded to look for a country retreat for herself. After staying with friends in Berkshire and Hertfordshire, she and Adrian spent a week over Christmas near the Sussex coast where she found a house, on the South Downs at Firle, not far from Lewes. She rented it, naming it Little Talland House, and in the new year began to furnish it. It was early in the new year that she met a group of young women who were to become important in her life. Marjorie Strachey was another of Lytton's sisters, and closer to him emotionally than Pernel, who was a member of the Friday Club. Marjorie and Virginia were the same age but, unlike Virginia, Marjorie had attended school and studied at Somerville College, Oxford. She was active in the campaign for women's suffrage. With Marjorie, whom Virginia already knew, were the two Costelloe sisters, Karin and Rachel - known as 'Ray', also an active suffragist - and Katherine Cox, universally known as 'Ka'.

Neo-Pagans, Ka Cox and Rupert Brooke, camping in 1911.

Random House, London

Vanessa and Virginia referred to this group and a number of their friends as the 'Neo-Pagans'. The Costelloe sisters and Ka had been educated at Newnham College, Cambridge (when Pernel Strachey was teaching there). Ka was five years Virginia's junior, and had gained a degree in history the previous year. In April and again in May 1911, Virginia invited Ka and Ray to her new house and, in August, Virginia was to join Ka and her friends on a camping expedition. Between these meetings, Virginia travelled to Turkey. Vanessa had gone there with Clive, Roger Fry and Harry Norton, a friend they had got to know through Lytton. She was pregnant and unwell when they set out; whilst there she had a miscarriage and her physical and mental condition deteriorated. Clive wrote reassuring letters to Virginia but they only convinced her to travel to see her sister. Doubtless, memories of the disastrous 1906 holiday in Greece influenced her decision. In the interim, Roger Fry had taken charge of the situation and he and Vanessa had fallen in love. Although this was not openly acknowledged it was apparent to Virginia. They all returned to London on the Orient Express, but being home did not improve matters greatly for Vanessa, who remained depressed and physically unwell long after the journey. Throughout this time, Virginia continued to write her first novel, the crisis of which focuses on the heroine becoming unwell when abroad and in love.

In July, Leonard Woolf, who had just returned on leave from Ceylon, dined with Clive and Vanessa. He and Clive had been friends at Cambridge, and they were joined after dinner by another Cambridge friend, Walter Lamb, and by Duncan Grant and Virginia. What Virginia did not know was that Lytton, shortly after he had proposed to her, had written to Leonard Woolf about the fiasco, adding, 'I think there's no doubt whatever that you ought to marry her...If you came and proposed she'd accept. She really would.' Leonard's half-facetious reply had been: 'wire to me if she accepts. I'll take the next boat home.' Leonard had gained his sexual experience in Ceylon, and had contemplated a future in that country with a Sinhalese wife. He had had the most fleeting of contacts with his friend Thoby's sister and, although he had been struck by her beauty, once far away in Ceylon he had almost forgotten her. Lytton, having once planted the suggestion of marriage to Virginia, cultivated it in his friend's mind. By August 1909 Lytton was writing:

> *Your destiny is clearly marked out for you, but will you allow it to work? You must marry Virginia. She's sitting waiting for you, is there any objection? She's the only woman in the world with sufficient brains: it's a miracle that she should exist; but if you're not careful you'll lose the opportunity. At any moment she might go off with heaven knows who Duncan? Quite possible. She's young, wild, inquisitive, discontented, and longing to be in love. If I were you I should telegraph. But at any rate come and see her before the end of 1910.*

It was almost another year before Leonard Woolf would 'come and see her', and in that year he thought of her a great deal, coming to believe that marrying her was 'the only way to happiness'. He reappeared in Virginia's life at a time when the lease on her London house was coming to an end, and she and Adrian were considering moving to a larger Bloomsbury house and sharing it with friends. Virginia had agonized over a proposal from one of her deceased brother's friends, but she had decided to remain unmarried. She was about to agonize over another. Shortly after meeting Leonard at Gordon Square, Virginia accepted Walter Lamb's invitation to join him on a 'great expedition' in Richmond Park. Afterwards, she wrote a long letter to her sister about the expedition, on which Walter had made a convoluted half-proposal of marriage to her. She told Vanessa that he had asked, 'Do you want to have children & love in the normal way?' and had gone on to say, 'I do care for you very much...marriage is so difficult - Will you let me wait?'

Vanessa, who was convalescing, had other things on her mind. Virginia visited her, after first spending two days with Janet Case. August was a month of much socializing for Virginia. She spent a few days with Ottoline and Philip Morrell, then almost a week with the poet Rupert Brooke, thought by all who met him to be 'beautiful', at his home in Grantchester. Like Ka Cox, with whom he had a prolonged affair, he was five years younger than Virginia and a Neo-Pagan. Entering into the Neo-Pagan spirit, Virginia bathed naked by moonlight with Brooke and, later that month, camped out with him, Ka, the economist Maynard Keynes - who was nearer in age to Virginia and lived with Duncan Grant in Fitzroy Square - and a number of others. There was, it seems, no romance or sexual intimacy between Virginia and Rupert Brooke. Although he would not ask Ka to marry him, he was attached to her more than to any other woman. He had a nervous breakdown the following year, having fallen out with all in the Bloomsbury circle except Virginia, to whom he wrote whilst he was still unwell.

Between her two holidays with Rupert Brooke, Virginia also spent time at Little Talland House, with the two servants who had worked for her and her brother Adrian in London. She had invited Leonard Woolf to visit her at Firle shortly after they met in July. He had had to refuse her first invitation but joined Marjorie Strachey and Desmond MacCarthy on a visit to her in September at what she now called her 'hideous suburban villa' in Firle. The weekend was a success: Leonard and Virginia enjoyed each other's company, and with him she discovered a new place to live in Sussex - Asheham. The following week, Virginia went to visit Vanessa at Studland and they agreed to take the lease of Asheham together. Once back in London, she was also arranging the move from 29 Fitzroy Square to 38 Brunswick Square.

November 1911 was a busy month. Although much caught up in arrangements for moving to two new houses, Virginia saw Leonard often, and managed also to spend sufficient time with Sydney Waterlow for him to declare his love to her. She had first met him over a year before at Studland with his now-estranged wife. She did not give an immediate answer to his proposal but wrote, shortly after Leonard's move into Brunswick Square, to tell Sydney that she could not return his love. Leonard arranged that he would take up residence on the top floor of the Brunswick Square house shortly after Virginia, Adrian, Duncan and Maynard had moved there. These arrangements were easily made and suited Virginia well, but they were socially very daring, and her old friend Violet Dickinson told her as much. Although she valued Violet's friendship, it was through this incident that Virginia realized Violet's approval was no longer essential to her. George Duckworth also expressed his disapproval, but George's view was of even less account than Violet's. Virginia had made her plans, and they were carried through, so that by the end of 1911, the intended establishment was in place.

Opposite page:

Virginia and Rupert Brooke, in Devon.

National Portrait Gallery, London

'On the Roof at Brunswick Square' by Duncan Grant, 1912. Adrian is seated between Virginia and Leonard, who were soon to be married. Although Maynard Keynes was also sharing the house, living with Duncan, he was not soaking up the sun on the roof when Duncan painted the picture.

© 1978 Estate of Duncan Grant, courtesy of Henrietta Garnett/ Bridgeman Art Library

Just over a month after moving into Brunswick Square, Leonard went to stay with a friend in Somerset. Once there, he decided to travel back to London for one day - to propose marriage to Virginia. She did not accept immediately. They exchanged letters; Virginia's said, 'I should like to go on as before; & (that) you should leave me free'. During the month following Leonard's proposal, she visited Vanessa on the Isle of Wight and there were two house-warming parties at Asheham. Whatever equilibrium Virginia might have been experiencing began to topple in that month. By mid-February, she was back with Jean Thomas in Twickenham. Leonard's leave from his post in Ceylon was running out and he requested an extension. His anxiety about his work made him perhaps more pressing in his need for a definite reply from Virginia. His letters were long and rambling; he was clearly a man passionately in love and wanting a positive end to his uncertainty.

Virginia took just over four months before agreeing to marry Leonard Woolf. From Miss Thomas's nursing home she spent time at Asheham with family and friends, as well as Leonard. Ka Cox was with her at Asheham a good deal and was to become an important friend to Virginia at this stage of her life. When Virginia was in London, sharing her new home with Leonard, her brother and friends, she got to know Leonard better and began to value him more and more. Before he received a definite 'yes' from her, Leonard resigned his Colonial Office post. When in Ceylon, he had bought a winning ticket for the local sweepstake, an equivalent of the modern National Lottery. He had no inheritance from his father, who had been a senior barrister - a Queen's Counsel - and who had died suddenly leaving a large family with almost no money when Leonard was 11 years old. Therefore, from an early age Leonard had had first-hand knowledge of economic insecurity. Scholarships had supported him through school and university. When he proposed to Virginia he had just over £500. Owing to the legacies left to her on the deaths of her half-sister, brother and aunt, and the sale of Sir Leslie's property, Virginia had an annual income of £400. She had supplemented this with her journalism. At 38 Brunswick Square, both Leonard and Virginia wrote in order to earn money. 'Her novel languishes I fear,' wrote Clive in a letter at this time. Leonard became a writer, and was active in left-wing politics, but at the time of proposing to Virginia, he had very uncertain prospects.

Leonard's financial position was not as important as a number of other factors. Virginia, in one of her letters to him, explained straightforwardly that she felt 'no physical attraction' to him, and the strength of his desire made her 'angry'. When Leonard had been in Ceylon, Lytton had written that Virginia's name reflected the degree of her sexual experience: she was a virgin. One reason for her anger surely lay in her relationships with her half-brothers. Nearly twenty years after writing of George's advances, she wrote of a much earlier experience with her other half-brother, Gerald. Two years before she died, Virginia wrote *A Sketch of the Past*, which begins with the words, 'Two days ago - Sunday 16th April 1939 to be precise - Nessa said that if I did not start writing my memoirs I should soon be too old.' And so it was at Vanessa's instigation that Virginia reached back into her childhood for some explanation of the woman she had become. She recalled Talland House in St Ives and her self-consciousness in looking at herself in a mirror in the hall there. She concluded that

Leonard and Adrian (and an unnamed dog in the upstairs window) at Asheham House.

Random House, London

> *I must have been ashamed or afraid of my own body. Another memory, also of the hall, may help to explain this. There was a slab outside the dining room door for standing dishes upon. Once when I was very small Gerald Duckworth lifted me onto this, and as I sat there he began to explore my body. I can remember the feel of his hand going under my clothes; going firmly and steadily lower and lower. I remember how I hoped that he would stop; how I stiffened and wriggled as his hand approached my private parts. But it did not*

> *stop. His hand explored my private parts too. I remember resenting, disliking*
> *it - what is the word for so dumb and mixed a feeling? It must have been*
> *strong, since I still recall it.*

In the light of this, Virginia's telling Leonard that she felt 'angry sometimes at
the strength of your desire' is more explicable. Leonard was, in many respects,
extremely patient, writing that Virginia need not make a decision about marriage
until she had finished her novel. She was rewriting it, having felt dissatisfied with the
first drafts. Vanessa, visiting Italy with Clive and Roger Fry, wrote to Virginia, 'Don't
have another breakdown. I don't believe you *can* both work and fall in love.'
Throughout Leonard's courtship of Virginia, Vanessa was supportive of their
marrying. She appreciated the depth of Leonard's feelings and felt he would be
exactly the type of husband for her fragile sister. The tremor from which he had
suffered from a very early age, and which was affected by stress, might suggest that
his nervous system was fragile and that he was perhaps not a suitable partner. Vanessa
saw that this was not the case: his tremor was of no consequence, his character was
fundamentally sound, and his attachment to Virginia undeniable. Clive had a
somewhat different opinion of Leonard. His view was doubtless clouded by a degree
of jealousy, but also by a residual anti-Semitism. He also perceived Leonard's interest
in Virginia as an intrusion upon the prolonged flirtation that he had established with
his sister-in-law.

The freedom with which people at the beginning of the century made what
we now consider racist remarks might be shocking to some readers. Desmond
MacCarthy's wife, Molly - with whom Clive had an affair - received a letter in which
Clive quite unselfconsciously wrote, without specifying his feeling, of 'what none of
us can help feeling for Jews'. He felt that Leonard was 'quite a good fellow', adding,
'he's a Jew you know'. Virginia herself described Leonard to Violet Dickinson as a
'penniless Jew' after they had become engaged.

Together, Virginia and Leonard visited their respective family and friends.
Virginia was perplexed by aspects of Mrs Woolf's Jewish orthodoxy, and felt herself
in an alien environment only five miles or so from Bloomsbury. For his part,
Leonard could not understand some of Virginia's attachments – to Madge

Vaughan, for example. Clive, to use Vanessa's word, 'resented' Virginia's engagement more than Vanessa's affair with Roger Fry. And he was not alone in being offended. None of Leonard's family was present when, on 10 August 1912, Virginia, aged 30, and Leonard, aged 31, were married at St Pancras Town Hall. A thunderstorm raged outside.

Virginia and Leonard after their engagement; photographed by George Duckworth on 23 July 1912, at his home, Dalingridge Place.

Tate Gallery Archive

❧ *Voyages Out*

Following their wedding and the gathering at Gordon Square afterwards, Virginia and Leonard stayed in Sussex at Asheham. The honeymoon proper was to take place abroad, but they also visited Somerset before setting out for France, Spain and Italy. They did not return to London for almost seven weeks. During their travels, each read a great deal as well as writing letters home, where there was much curiosity about their sex life. On arrival in England, they stayed at 38 Brunswick Square for a week before moving to eighteenth-century rooms at 13 Clifford's Inn. This establishment was even more like Cambridge college life than any of the Bloomsbury homes. A porter and cleaner were employed by all of the tenants of the tall building and, after some disasterous attempts at cooking, Virginia and Leonard chose to eat out at the nearby Cock Tavern. Leonard had work as Secretary to Roger Fry's second Post-Impressionist Exhibition from October to January 1913, and by November he had finished his novel, *The Village in the Jungle*. Virginia worked on redrafting her novel. When Leonard wrote of the early years of their marriage in his autobiography, he recalled that during these first months

> *she was finishing* The Voyage Out, *writing every day with a kind of tortured intensity. I did not know then what over the years we learnt bitterly by experience, that the weeks or months in which she finished a book would always be a terrific mental and nervous strain upon her and bring her to the verge of a mental breakdown. It was not merely the strain of the mental intensity with which she always wrote, the artistic integrity and ruthlessness which made her drive herself remorselessly towards perfection. She also suffered from… an almost pathological hypersensitiveness to criticism, so that she suffered an ever increasingly agonizing nervous apprehension as she got nearer and nearer to the end of her book and the throwing of it and of herself to the critics.*

In the case of *The Voyage Out*, Virginia's sensitivity was further tried by her submitting the novel to Gerald Duckworth, for publication by his publishing house, the Duckworth Press. Between Leonard's finishing his novel and Virginia's finishing hers, the couple both fell ill, though from different causes. Leonard's susceptibility to malaria had been triggered by their travels and his condition worsened during December. Virginia's health was beginning to decline in the way it had done before and would again. In the new year, Vanessa visited the Woolfs at Asheham and wrote of her sister, 'she has in reality amazing courage & sanity about life. I have seen so little of her lately that it has struck me here.' Virginia's fundamental sanity persisted, throughout her life, even up to the brink of her periods of illness. As Hermione Lee has written in her biography of Virginia,

> *Virginia Woolf was a sane woman who had an illness. She was often a patient,*
> *but she was not a victim. She was not weak, or hysterical, or self-deluding, or*
> *guilty, or oppressed. On the contrary, she was a person of exceptional courage,*
> *intelligence and stoicism, who made the best use she could, and came to the*
> *deepest understanding possible to her, of her own condition. She endured,*
> *periodically, great agony of mind and severe physical pain, with remarkably*
> *little self-pity.*

One of those periods of great agony of mind was coming now. Although unwell himself, Leonard Woolf was aware of the precarious nature of Virginia's health at the end of 1912. Early in 1913 he began to keep a record of her condition, and sought medical advice concerning the advisability of their having children. Violet Dickinson had given a cradle as her wedding gift, and the Woolfs (often referred to by family and friends as 'the Woolves') had hoped to be parents. Leonard began to consult doctors, Jean Thomas and Vanessa on the advisability of Virginia's bearing children. He received conflicting responses, some thinking that rest in the country would improve her health, others expressing doubts that she would ever be sufficiently stable to be a mother. So, in the early months of 1913 Virginia and Leonard spent time with family and friends away from London.

The manuscript of *The Voyage Out* was in Gerald Duckworth's hands in early March, a month in which Virginia joined Leonard in travelling about to and from towns and cities in the north of England. He was gathering an understanding of the Co-operative movement - a democratic organization, founded by working people

Margaret Llewelyn Davies and Leonard Woolf, Co-operative Movement companions, resting during a walk in Cornwall, 1916.

Random House, London

initially to provide affordable goods and share profits. Margaret Llewelyn Davies, whom Virginia and Leonard met through Janet Case, organized the Women's Co-operative Guild (WCG). As a socialist, Leonard began to take an interest in this organization for working-class women. He and Virginia visited meetings at which he spoke of the value of collective work. Later in the year they would attend the WCG Congress and get to know Beatrice and Sidney Webb, leading lights of the Fabian Society. This organization had been founded in 1884 by socialists who believed in gradual reform by the patient, persistent use of argument. Members arranged annual conferences, and Virginia and Leonard attended the one held in July 1913. Interspersed between these political meetings were purely social gatherings at Asheham and in London. Virginia experienced the agony of correcting proofs of her novel and, by the time of the Fabian Society Conference, her health was on the point of collapse. They returned to London and, on her doctor's advice, Virginia resentfully went to Twickenham for a rest-cure.

From this point, numerous cures were attempted but Virginia's condition spiralled downward. She returned home from Twickenham. A doctor advised the couple to return to the Somerset inn of their honeymoon. Ka Cox joined them there at Leonard's request. Virginia was in a poor state physically and mentally: she was not eating, could not sleep and was experiencing delusions. Accompanied by Ka, the couple returned to Adrian's rooms in Brunswick Square, where doctors were consulted and Vanessa was called. Leonard and Vanessa left Virginia with Ka whilst they went to another doctor.

Once they were gone Virginia took an overdose of the sleeping drug, veronal, which Leonard had left unlocked in his luggage. Ka found her in a profound sleep, rang Leonard and, only through the swift action of Maynard Keynes's brother,

Geoffrey, who was a hospital doctor living on the top floor at 38 Brunswick Square, was Virginia's stomach pumped, and her life saved.

Virginia's mental and physical health did not fully improve until the end of 1915. During the fourteen months from suicide attempt to life without medical attention, Virginia moved, or was moved, from place to place, sometimes accompanied by as many as four nurses. She and Leonard gave up their rooms in Clifford's Inn and made their permanent home in Richmond, Surrey. Immediately following her overdose, she was moved to one of George Duckworth's houses in Sussex to be looked after by two nurses. Two months later, the move to Asheham was made. Here Ka helped to care for her. Leonard had to spend time in London arranging their moving out of Clifford's Inn towards the end of the year, and at the beginning of the 1914 he visited Lytton Strachey. His own health, both mental and physical, had taken a battering and he needed a rest-cure himself. Janet Case, Vanessa and Ka all helped to care for Virginia while he was away.

By April Virginia was considered sufficiently well to leave Asheham for three weeks in Cornwall. She had been living very quietly, reading, writing letters and typing for Leonard. His novel *The Wise Virgins* was published in the spring. In Cornwall, she came into contact with people neither of them knew, and both experienced a degree of stress but the journey contributed to a recovery of sorts. Back in Asheham, when Leonard was away from home at conferences, there was what Vanessa described to Clive as an accidental taking of veronal, but the dose merely resulted in a long sleep. Virginia began to contemplate returning to London, a prospect that caused Leonard considerable concern. He was convinced that London life contributed in good measure to nervous excitement in Virginia, and this was a condition he was anxious should be avoided. War was declared in August; however, the patriotic frenzy that gripped much of the nation had little or no impact on Virginia. She and Leonard spent one night in London but travelled on to Northumberland, returning to Asheham at the end of September. Within less than a month, having looked for a London house, they had moved to lodgings at Richmond, and Virginia attended cookery classes. Lytton entertained them at his home in Wiltshire the following month, and they spent Christmas near him, Virginia seeming to have made a full recovery.

At the beginning of 1915, Virginia began to keep a diary, to write her second novel, *Night and Day*, and to contemplate the reception of her first, which was to appear in March. She and Leonard began to plan their move to another house in Richmond, Hogarth House. In letters, her mood was lively and effusive. She wrote to Margaret Llewelyn Davies towards the end of February, thanking her for supporting Leonard in his political work during her illness. In the days following her letters to Margaret, the liveliness of Virginia's conversation rapidly became manic. She became over-excited and began to speak gibberish. With the help of nurses, Leonard took care of her until he could arrange the move to Hogarth House. Whilst he supervised the move, Virginia was in a nursing home, and it was then that *The Voyage Out* was published. Virginia came to live in Hogarth House accompanied by four nurses whom she grew to loathe. Her loathing made her violent, and her strongest animosity was reserved for Leonard. Although living in the same house, he saw little of her during the first two months they were there together. This period was followed by an improvement in Virginia's health, but her spirits were little better. Ka, who visited Virginia at this time, reported to Vanessa that 'she won't see Leonard at all & has taken against all men'.

As the summer progressed, Virginia gradually improved. She began reading, and wrote postcards to friends. In spite of her general improvement and imminent return to Asheham, she despaired over her future as a writer: 'what's the use of my writing novels?' she wrote to Margaret. What she could not know at this stage of her life was how she would call up these very experiences in writing her later novels. Her childhood response of feeling 'nothing whatever', before her first breakdown when her mother died, would become part of Septimus Warren Smith's response to death in *Mrs Dalloway*. The same character, when experiencing his breakdown, believed 'love between man and woman was repulsive to Shakespeare. The business of copulation was filth to him before the end.' Virginia, after returning to Asheham, which she and Leonard had rented to the newly married Sydney Waterlow and his wife during the previous year, wrote to Lytton that Sydney 'proposes to live next door to us at Richmond and there copulate day and night and produce 6 little Waterlows. This house for a long time stank to me of dried semen.'

Leonard, in caring for Virginia, was supported by a nurse, as well as a cook and housemaid. The cost of Virginia's treatment caused him some worry, but he was glad that she was sleeping and eating as the doctors wished. She was now over 40 pounds heavier than her accustomed weight as a result of the recommended diet, which included quantities of milk - as did the preferred cure of the eminent doctor-villain in *Mrs Dalloway*, who ordered:

rest in bed; rest in solitude; silence and rest; rest without friends, without books, without messages; six months' rest; until a man who went in weighing seven stone six comes out weighing twelve.

Virginia now weighed twelve stone (168 lbs), and had a profound mistrust of doctors. She had learned from her experience that she and Leonard knew more about her condition than did any doctor. In years to come she was to refer to this period of illness in a letter to her friend, the composer Ethel Smyth:

As to seeing a doctor who will cure my headaches, no, Ethel No. And whats more you will seriously upset L, if you suggest it. We spent I daresay a hundred pounds when it meant selling my few rings and necklaces to pay them, without any more result than that if I get a pain, go to bed, and eat meat it goes. No other cure has ever been found - and the disease - well, all the nerves meet in the spine: its simple enough. No complicated mysteries about my headaches.

From Asheham, the household moved back to Hogarth House in November and, shortly after the move, Leonard dispensed with the services of the nurse. Virginia was well enough at Christmas for them to invite Lytton's youngest brother, James, and Noel Olivier to stay. It was the second Christmas of the Great War and Rupert Brooke had died of blood poisoning in the spring of 1915, when Virginia's mental condition had been at its worst. Noel had been loved by both Rupert Brooke and Virginia's brother Adrian (who had married in 1914 one of Virginia's Neo-Pagan friends, Karin Costelloe, when the Woolfs moved to Richmond). Noel's affair with James Strachey lasted for more than twenty years, although James would be married

Letter to James Strachey from Virginia, giving directions to Hogarth House, with a map provided by Leonard.

British Library, Additional MS 60734, folios 129 and 129 verso

to another woman within five years. Although the marriage between Virginia and Leonard had been severely shaken by Virginia's illness, it was still intact, and became stronger as the years went on. Amongst their friends, infidelity was almost commonplace. Vanessa's life was to change radically in the coming year, when she began an uncomfortable *ménage à trois* in Suffolk with Duncan Grant and David (nicknamed 'Bunny') Garnett, a childhood friend of Noel Olivier.

Vanessa's erstwhile lover, Roger Fry, began to take a place of importance in Virginia's life from the Christmas of 1915, and he stayed in Hogarth House early in 1916 when working on a commission at the nearby Hampton Court. Her discussions with him about form in art and literature influenced her writing, although not until some time later. More material concerns were uppermost in the Woolfs' minds at this time, and other important relationships were to be forged. At his home in Guildford, Roger Fry had employed two women who now came to work for Virginia and

Leonard as cook and housemaid, Nelly Boxall and Lottie Hope. The relationship between Virginia and her servants was to be a stormy one, but Lottie stayed with the Woolfs for eight years, and Nelly for eighteen.

The Great War, which many had predicted would 'be over by Christmas' when it had begun in August 1914, had on the contrary continued until the next Christmas and was affecting everyone's lives by early 1916, when conscription was introduced. To avoid being called up, Duncan and Bunny had taken up farming in Suffolk. A tribunal decided that their self-employed status prevented their exemption from military service, and so, with Vanessa, they moved to Charleston, near Asheham, in Sussex to be employed by a farmer. Clive and Adrian, both conscientious objectors, also worked on farms, although Clive appears to have spent much of his time on Ottoline Morrell's husband's farm doing very little farm-work. Philip Morrell, an MP, had been one of the few politicians to object to the declaration of war, and employed a number of artists and writers as farm-workers - to his economic disadvantage. Leonard had been medically exempted from war service. His tremor, and Virginia's need of him, had secured a certificate of unfitness. Two of his brothers were less fortunate: Philip was wounded by a shell that killed their brother, Cecil. Lytton was also exempted on medical grounds.

Nelly Boxall (left), the Woolfs' cook, and Lottie Hope, their housemaid, at Charleston with Vanessa and Duncan's daughter (who was named Angelica Bell).

Tate Gallery Archive

53

⤳ *Recovery*

Virginia took up her social and writing life again in 1916. She suffered a bout of influenza, but was otherwise well, and by the end of the year she had published fifteen articles and reviews. She and Leonard entertained friends at Asheham, and were entertained by friends, including the Webbs and George Bernard Shaw and his wife. They also visited Vanessa in Suffolk and, in September, returned to Cornwall for a holiday. From October Virginia began her four-year association with the Women's Co-operative Guild in Richmond. Meetings took place each month at Hogarth House, and Virginia organized a series of talks to be given by her brilliant and well-travelled friends. One talk, on the danger to soldiers of sexually transmitted diseases, thoroughly shocked and upset the local women but, as Virginia wrote, they 'recanted' and asked for a speaker on sex education, thus making Virginia feel that she was engaged in really worthwhile work.

Katherine Mansfield, 1920. Virginia wrote, 'I was jealous of her writing – the only writing I have ever been jealous of.'

Random House, London

Earlier in October, two women art students, Dora Carrington and Barbara Hiles, began to feature in the Woolfs' lives. Carrington, known to all simply by her surname, was sharing a Bloomsbury house with another painter, Dorothy Brett, and the writers Katherine Mansfield and John Middleton Murry. Virginia had heard of Katherine Mansfield from Lytton, and Katherine had read and admired *The Voyage Out*, but it was several months between Lytton's mentioning her and her meeting Virginia.

Katherine Mansfield was six years younger than Virginia and different from her in many ways. She had been born in New Zealand and then educated in London between the ages of 15 and 18. She had returned to New Zealand to train as a secretary and write for local newspapers for two unhappy years before leaving for London again in 1908. There she fell in love with one man and became pregnant, married another man and left him shortly after the wedding. She gave birth to a stillborn child in Germany, and then, having again become pregnant, this time by her husband, she had an abortion. Her relationship with John Middleton Murry began in 1911, the year in which her first collection of short stories was published. She and Murry were to live together and separate, take other lovers, marry and periodically live apart, partly sustained by other relationships, until Katherine died of tuberculosis near Paris in 1923. Her illness first appeared after her abortion and was initially diagnosed as pleurisy. If in nothing else, Virginia and Katherine shared ill-luck in their doctors. In fact, suffering ill-health contributed to the bond that developed between them. When Katherine died, Virginia made a long entry in her diary, near the end of which she wrote, 'I think I never gave her credit for all her physical suffering & the effect it must have had in embittering her.'

In that same diary entry, in January 1923, Virginia considered the complexity of her feeling for Katherine, and acknowledged the other's importance in her life. There had been a rivalry between them as writers: 'I was jealous of her writing - the only writing I have ever been jealous of. This made it harder to write to her'. Yet there had been friendship too:

> Sometimes we looked very steadfastly at each other, as though we had reached some durable relationship, independent of the changes of the body, through the eyes... Most days I think we reached that kind of certainty, in talk about books, or rather about our writings, which I thought had something durable about it. And then she was inscrutable. Did she care for me? Sometimes she would say so - would kiss me - would look at me as if (is this sentiment?) her eyes would like always to be faithful. She would promise never never to forget. That was what we said at the end of our last talk. She said she would send me her diary to read, & would write always. For our friendship was a real thing we said, looking at each other quite straight. It would always go on whatever happened. What happened was, I suppose, faultfindings & perhaps gossip. She never answered my

letter. Yet I still feel, somehow that friendship persists. Still there are things about writing I think of & want to tell Katherine.

Mandrill holding the arm of her Mongoose at Studland.

Dr Milo Keynes

When Virginia wrote this entry, she was a successful published writer. When Katherine had been alive, Virginia had experienced a sense of fellowship with her; although quite unlike her in numerous ways, Katherine was another woman for whom writing was the most important thing in her life. Katherine was always conscious that, in Murry, she lacked the love and support Virginia received from her husband. For, whatever Vanessa, Clive and others said and wrote about the lack of sexual compatibility between Virginia and Leonard, there existed a deep love. When this was expressed they often used the affectionate names they adopted, as Mandrill (Virginia) and Mongoose (Leonard). Recovering from influenza in April 1916, Virginia had written to her 'Precious Mongoose', ending with:

Thats all my news, but I lie and think of my precious beast, who does make me more happy every day and instant of my life than I thought it possible to be. There's no doubt I'm terribly in love with you. I keep thinking what you're doing, and have to stop - it makes me want to kiss you so...It will be joyful to see your dear funny face tomorrow.

The Marmots kiss you.

Yr <u>*MANDRILL*</u>

These affectionate names were not 'baby' names: the mandrill, according to the Oxford English Dictionary, is 'the largest, most hideous, and most ferocious of the baboons'; and the mongoose, although small, is weasel- or ferret-like and able to kill venomous snakes unharmed. Freud, whom Leonard read first in 1914 and whose works were later published by the Hogarth Press, might have made some interesting observations on these names.

Following Virginia's resumption of writing of fiction and journalism in 1916, the Woolfs acquired a printing press. They had talked of buying a press more than two years before, on Virginia's thirty-third birthday in 1915, but her illness and slow recovery had postponed the purchase until March 1917 and its installation until late April that year. It was delivered to their Richmond home and thus was named the Hogarth Press when they produced their first publication in July. Working on the press thoroughly absorbed both Virginia and Leonard. It proved to be exactly the sort of 'therapy' Leonard had intended it to be, for Virginia in type-setting, and for Leonard in machining. Before she had married, Virginia had learned book binding. She and Leonard now taught themselves from an instruction book how to set up and print on their small handpress.

Their first production was a slim volume of two stories, *The Mark on the Wall* by Virginia and *Three Jews* by Leonard. In Virginia's story there is evidence of her discussions with Roger Fry during the previous year. The narrator recalls and re-enacts considering a mark on her wall, recording that her perceptions change as she views it from different directions. In dwelling upon it, she is able to 'sink deeper and deeper, away from the surface'. The work is more reverie than conventional story. Lytton considered it a 'work of genius', going on to say in a letter to Leonard that the 'liquidity of style fills me with envy: really some of the sentences! - How on earth does she make the English language float and float?' Vanessa pleased Virginia by praising it and adding, 'I shouldn't think you had much to fear from the rivalry of Katherine Mansfield & Co'. Virginia had been too ill on the publication of *The Voyage Out* to enjoy what had been generally good reviews; she therefore relished these responses - and the profit of just over £7 that the initial print run of 134 copies made.

Towards the end of the first year of the Hogarth Press, Madge Vaughan's sister-in-law Emma gave them the equipment she had used for bookbinding, and they purchased second-hand a larger press and employed Bunny Garnett's friend Barbara Hiles as their first assistant. Establishing the press kept Virginia and Leonard in Richmond for much of the spring and early summer of 1917. Virginia more than doubled her previous year's output of reviews and articles and continued working on her 'exercise in the conventional style', her second novel. In August and

*Lytton and Carrington
reading Gibbon's* The
Decline & Fall of the
Roman Empire.

Random House, London

September they took a break from their work and went to Asheham, where Virginia resumed writing the diary which she had neglected since February 1915. Having resumed it, she was to maintain it for the rest of her life. Whilst at Asheham, Virginia and Leonard entertained several guests, including Katherine Mansfield, whose story, *Prelude*, they promised to publish. Lytton was also one of their guests. He was accompanied by Philip Morrell, who reciprocated the Woolfs' hospitality by inviting them to Garsington Manor for a weekend in November. Lytton was there too, and it was at around this time that he began living with Carrington. Although Carrington had lovers and, indeed, married in 1921, she adored Lytton and they lived together in an asexual relationship for the rest of their lives.

Before the year was over, Leonard was instrumental in establishing the 1917 Club. Old Bloomsbury met a younger group of people in Gerrard Street, Soho, initially out of a mutual interest in socialism. Leonard had, for many years, been actively involved in left-wing politics, both in Fabian Society and Labour Party policy-making and in writing. He specialized in international relations, writing a number of influential articles and books on international as well as domestic politics. When Leonard and Virginia had separate business in London, they would meet in Gerrard Street. In 1917, the war continued and there were air raids from that autumn. The new year once more brought hope for peace and a law giving women over thirty the right to vote and to sit in parliament. Virginia's second novel was taking up much of her time and, in spite of another period in bed with influenza, she had produced more than 100,000 words by March 1918. The novel's conventionality contrasted strongly with Katherine Mansfield's *Prelude* - which, because of its length, Virginia took a long time to set - and contrasted too with the first chapters of a novel that was brought to them the following month: *Ulysses*, by James Joyce. They turned it down as, not only was it far too long for them to print, but also its content would undoubtedly have led to a prosecution for obscenity.

In May, Lytton's *Eminent Victorians* appeared. Virginia had been reading it during the years of its composition and, although entertained, she was not impressed. On its publication, nevertheless, its irreverent slant on such legendary figures as Cardinal Manning and Florence Nightingale was well received. The Woolfs spent a weekend in Oxfordshire with Lytton and Carrington, two months after *Eminent Victorians* appeared and shortly after publishing Katherine's *Prelude*. The visit to Lytton and Carrington's home marked the beginning of two-and-a-half months away from Richmond. During August and September they were at Asheham, as always, visited by family and friends. Shortly after their return to Richmond in October, Virginia's cousin Herbert Fisher, brother of Willy Fisher who had been embarrassed by the Dreadnought Hoax, brought news of the end of the war.

A few days after the November Armistice Day, an American poet who had lived in Bloomsbury, knew Ottoline and was working for a bank, brought some poems to Hogarth House. His name was T.S. Eliot. The Woolfs agreed to publish his poems and, thereafter, Eliot became a close friend. That same month, they finished printing Virginia's story *Kew Gardens* at around the same time that her second novel, *Night and Day*, was completed. Virginia's literary productivity was matched by her sister's on Christmas Day, 1918: Vanessa gave birth to a daughter, Angelica, the child of Duncan Grant. Vanessa remained married to Clive, who was living at Gordon Square and involved in an affair with Mrs Mary Hutchinson. Mary was fascinated by and became attached to Virginia, after a complex intrigue of the sort that Bloomsbury specialized in. She wrote to Lytton of the 'shabby grandeur' of Hogarth House, and 'thought V(irginia)'s charm was that she spoke sentences that one usually only finds written. Perfect literary sentences spoken without hesitation or stumbling.'

T.S. Eliot of whom a friend once remarked that his clothes were English but his underclothes were American.

Random House, London

*Clive and Mary
Hutchinson, 1922.*

Tate Gallery Archive

The first half of 1919 was taken up with domestic crises. First, Virginia had dental problems that kept her in bed for much of January; then Nelly Boxall was sent to Charleston to help Vanessa; and in the spring the owner of Asheham gave the Woolfs six months to find another country house. Writing articles, including *Modern Novels* (later retitled *Modern Fiction*) and printing at Hogarth House continued, however. Works by John Middleton Murry and T.S. Eliot were published at the same time as *Kew Gardens*. Virginia's novel, *Night and Day*, was too large to be a Hogarth Press production and so, reluctantly, Virginia submitted it to that 'pampered overfed pug dog', Gerald Duckworth, 'to be pawed and snored over by him'. Whilst she waited to hear if it had been accepted, and between its acceptance and publication in October that year, Virginia and Leonard looked for a new home in Sussex to replace Asheham. Unilaterally, Virginia bought a house in Lewes, not far from Asheham, before she and Leonard found Monk's House in Rodmell, a few miles from Asheham. They decided to sell the purchased house and instead buy Monk's House at auction. This they did in July, and moved their possessions there at the beginning of September. For the rest of their lives, Monk's House was to be the country home of Virginia and Leonard. Whenever they could they spent weekends, weeks and months there; and, when living in London became dangerous after the outbreak of war in 1939, they made it their principal home. Vanessa lived nearby at Charleston, and many friends and occasionally other members of the family visited them there.

Mixed with the pleasure of settling into the new house was the apprehension of the publication and dreaded reviews of *Night and Day*. Virginia sent a number of copies to family and friends, one of whom was the novelist E.M. Forster. He had been a Friday Club friend and guest of Ottoline, and was known to all by his middle name,

Morgan. 'I value Morgan's opinion as much as anybodies *(sic)*', she wrote in her diary, and when she considered his qualified admiration, and his reasons for having preferred *The Voyage Out*, recognized that his was 'not a criticism to discourage'. Katherine Mansfield's was another matter:

> *KM wrote a review which irritated me - I thought I saw spite in it. A decorous elderly dullard she describes me; Jane Austen up to date. Leonard supposes that she let her wish for my failure have its way with her pen...But what I perceive in all this is that praise hardly warms; blame stings far more keenly; & both are somehow at arms length.*

The stings would always hurt, and their hurt would always be dreaded. In the case of this novel, Katherine had found it 'interminable' and wrote several letters expressing her dread at having to review it. To Murry she wrote, 'it is a lie in the soul. The war never has been: that is what its message is'. Katherine's brother had been killed in the war that had just finished and she felt that Virginia had somehow betrayed her generation: 'the novel can't just leave the war out... I feel the *profoundest* sense that nothing can ever be the same - that, as artists, we are traitors if we feel otherwise: we have to take it into account and find new expressions, new moulds for our new thoughts and feelings.'

It had been that very newness that Virginia had been trying to avoid when writing *Night and Day*, a novel that centred on one young woman's defiance of her family and class when she married, and another young woman's renunciation of love in favour of the single life and fulfilment in work. With hindsight, Virginia wrote to Ethel Smyth:

The inscription reads 'Mr E.M. Forster in his full official robes at an Indian Court', and is signed and dated by the Maharaja of Dewas on 31 October, 1921.

King's College Library, Cambridge

> *I was so tremblingly afraid of my own insanity that I wrote Night and Day*
> *mainly to prove to my own satisfaction that I could keep entirely off that*
> *dangerous ground…Bad as the book is, it composed my mind, and I think taught*
> *me certain elements of composition which I should not have had the patience to*
> *learn had I been in full flush of health always.*

Virginia had little time to dwell upon Katherine's review. Leonard suffered another occurence of malaria and, no sooner had he recovered than Virginia took to her bed with influenza. Her birthday in January put her in a thoughtful frame of mind concerning her writing. The 'new' things that Katherine had lamented her novel had so lacked were very much in Virginia's mind. In the diary entry for the day following her thirty-eighth birthday, she expressed her happiness at having only that afternoon

> *arrived at some idea of a new form for a new novel. Suppose one thing should*
> *open out of another - as in An Unwritten Novel - only not for 10 pages but*
> *200 or so - doesn't that give the looseness & lightness I want: doesn't that get*
> *closer & yet keep form & speed, & enclose everything, everything? My doubt*
> *is how far it will enclose the human heart - Am I sufficiently mistress of*
> *my dialogue to net it there?*

This new type of novel was to become *Jacob's Room*, which she began writing in 1920 and published two years later. Alongside the novel, she wrote and had published articles and reviews - almost every month of 1920 - in the *Athenaeum*, *New Statesman* and *Times Literary Supplement*. American editions of *The Voyage Out*, which she revised, and *Night and Day* were published. During this year, Virginia was also writing the eight stories to be published the following year by the Hogarth Press as *Monday or Tuesday*. *The London Mercury* also published one of them, *An Unwritten Novel*. In this story, the narrator observes a woman on a train, and constructs her life-story with great conviction - only to be proved utterly wrong at the end of the journey. The narrator is delighted rather than dismayed by the unpredictable outcome.

Virginia's social life of visiting and being visited was given a new focus in the spring of this year by the establishment of the Memoir Club. Molly MacCarthy was its leading light, 'secretary and drudge'. Like an earlier but abortive creation of hers, the Novel Club, it was formed in the hope that her husband, Desmond, would give his brilliant conversation a more substantial form. The club met once a month and, after dining together, its members - Virginia and other 'Bloomsberries', as Molly called them, and a few more recent friends - would gather in one home or another to read autobiographical pieces.

Leonard's political work was taking up more of his time and, in May 1920, he was invited to stand for parliament as the Labour Party candidate representing the Seven Universities Democratic Association. In his autobiography, Leonard explains that 'there was a Combined English University Constituency which included all the English universities other than Cambridge and Oxford; they elected two MPs'. Despite his feeling that the 'business life of a backbench MP in the 1920s seemed to me the acme of futility and boredom', he accepted the invitation. This development in Leonard's life inevitably had some effect on Virginia's, although she continued to see friends, including Katherine Mansfield for the last time, and invite people to stay at Monk's House. Two of those guests were Carrington and Ralph Partridge, who

Carrington and Ralph Partridge.

King's College Library, Cambridge

were lovers at that time. Although Virginia and Leonard were taking a two-month holiday from Hogarth House, they were conscious that their writing and political commitments would take them away from working on the press themselves. Carrington's friend Barbara Hiles could not take on more responsibility and so Ralph was invited to work on the press.

Ralph - like the many young men who were, equally unsuccessfully, to follow him - was delighted at the prospect of working for the Woolfs three days a week. In practice, working for the Hogarth Press meant working for Leonard, who was not the most flexible of employers. Flexibility was not one of Ralph's characteristics, and so, although he worked hard, they inevitably came into conflict. His first major responsibility was the short story collection, *Monday or Tuesday*, published by the press in March 1921. Virginia's concern about reviews was altered on this occasion as Ralph, she believed, muddled the publication date and many journals failed to review it.

Virginia, on her part, also made the mistake of involving herself in Lytton, Carrington and Ralph's *ménage à trois* at Tidmarsh, which led to confusion, hurt feelings and Carrington's eventually marrying Ralph in May. In June Virginia began to experience symptoms that were all too familiar: 'wearisome headache, jumping pulse, aching back, frets, fidgets, lying awake, sleeping draughts, sedatives, digitalis, going for a little walk, and plunging back into bed again - all the horrors of the dark cupboard of illness once more displayed for my diversion'- as she described them in her 8 August diary entry, after two months of silence.

The 'severe bout' as Leonard described it in his autobiography, lasted two months, most of which were spent at Monk's House. Virginia's recovery took another two months, during which she was able to write, which contributed to an improvement in her spirits. In October she was back in Richmond, and by early November she was involved as much as ever in seeing friends. Earlier in the year she had accompanied Leonard on a trip to give a speech at Manchester University, where he flabbergasted the professors by saying that he did not wish to be elected. Virginia had found the experience depressing overall and so, when he had further political business to do in Manchester and Durham in December, Virginia did not join him.

The now almost predictable bout of influenza that gripped Virginia in January and February 1922 led to almost a year of visits to medical consultants of one sort and another, each of whom diagnosed Virginia's illness as the one in which *he* was a specialist. In his autobiography, Leonard wrote:

> *It was a perpetual struggle to find the precarious balance of health for her among the strains and stresses of writing and society... But during the first seven months of 1922 she was off and on continually unwell or threatened with headaches. In March she started a temperature which the doctors took seriously and sent us on a fairly long odyssey through Harley Street and Wimpole Street which gave us a curious view of medical science and the tiptop Harley Street specialists... At our last interview with the last famous Harley Street specialist to whom we paid our three guineas, the great Dr Saintsbury, as he shook Virginia's hand, said to her: 'Equanimity - equanimity - practise equanimity, Mrs. Woolf'.*

This experience served as a form of research for Virginia's next novel. The character Clarissa Dalloway had first appeared in *The Voyage Out*. In the summer of 1922, the summer in which T.S. Eliot brought *The Waste Land* to Hogarth House,

Virginia was engaged in writing a short story based upon Mrs Dalloway buying gloves in Bond Street. By October, the story had 'branched into a book' in which doctors and their differing diagnoses would feature prominently. Indeed, the novel's Harley Street specialist would worship not equanimity but 'Proportion, divine proportion'. In her diary, Virginia noted that the novel would be 'a study of insanity & suicide: the world seen by the sane & the insane side by side... more close to the fact than Jacob'.

Jacob's Room was published by the Hogarth Press towards the end of October 1922. At last she was free of Gerald Duckworth's 'pawing and snoring'. The Woolfs had found an Edinburgh firm to print it for them. In this novel, she did not 'leave the war out', as Katherine had accused her of doing in *Night and Day*. In fact, her hero Jacob's surname is 'Flanders', and he dies fighting in the Great War. The novel is, in content, the chronological story of his short life of school, Cambridge, work and social life in London, affairs, travel, love and war. The narrative style is fragmentary. One reviewer described it as technically adroit but sterile. Several friends, including Morgan and Lytton, wrote about it enthusiastically, but Virginia commented in her last diary entry of October, 1922:

> *I don't want to be totting up compliments, & comparing reviews. I want to think out Mrs. Dalloway. I want to foresee this book better than the others, & get the utmost out of it. I expect I could have screwed Jacob up tighter if I had foreseen; but I had to make my path as I went.*

⬿ *Established Writer*

There was barely time for Virginia to absorb the responses to *Jacob's Room* before the mid-November General Election. Much to the relief of both Woolfs, Leonard failed to win the Universities' seat and 'normal' life could be resumed. Virginia had deliberately reduced her writing of articles and reviews for publication during the years 1921 and 1922. She had felt it was 'time to read like an expert' in order to produce what would become *The Common Reader*, two collections of essays in literary criticism. With this in mind, she planned and began a structured programme of reading and writing. Towards the end of the year she met another woman writer who 'writes 15 pages a day - has finished another book - publishes with Heinemanns - knows everyone', Vita Sackville-West. Virginia's friendship with Vita was to be one of the most important relationships of her life.

Thoughts of an old friend were to dominate Virginia's mind at the beginning of 1923. Katherine Mansfield died early in January. This news, and another bout of influenza following shortly after, created a sombre atmosphere in Hogarth House at the beginning of 1923. A new full-time employee, Marjorie Joad, joined the press, Ralph left, and Leonard was offered and accepted the literary editorship of *The Nation and Athenaeum*. Before Leonard took up the post, the Woolfs travelled to Spain to stay with Gerald Brenan, a young man they had met and whose character had impressed them during the previous summer. The trip had the desired effect upon Virginia's health and spirits. On returning home, she continued to write to Brenan, maintaining the literary discussions that had so stimulated her. Leonard took up his new post and, shortly afterwards, Virginia gave up her unpaid work of finding speakers for the Richmond Women's Co-operative Guild.

During 1923, Virginia was writing the first version of *Mr Bennett and Mrs Brown*, in which that elusive character, a woman on a train, appeared once more. In this essay, she argued against the limitations of English neo-realist novels by Arnold Bennett, John Galsworthy and H.G. Wells. Her first published version was revised for a lecture in Cambridge the following year, and tinkered with further for publication later in 1924 as *Character in Fiction*. The subject of character, especially her ability (or not) to create characters, occupied her thoughts a good deal whilst she

was writing *Mrs Dalloway*, the working title of which was 'The Hours', and reading for and writing *The Common Reader* during the summer. At the end of August, she wrote in her diary:

> *I'm thinking furiously about Reading and Writing. I have no time to describe my plans. I should say a good deal about The Hours, & my discovery; how I dig out beautiful caves behind my characters; I think that gives exactly what I want; humanity, humour, depth. The idea is that the caves shall connect.*

This entry was written in the middle of the Woolfs' two months' stay at Monk's House, where they entertained numerous visitors. A weekend spent in Dorset in September provided Virginia with an opportunity to 'observe Lydia as a type for Rezia'. Lydia Lopokova was a Russian ballet dancer who married Maynard Keynes two years later and was a model for one of the characters in *Mrs Dalloway*.

Opposite:

'Lady in a Red Hat': Vita Sackville-West, painted by William Strang.

Glasgow Museums: Art Gallery and Museum, Kelvingrove

Below:

The 'Mrs Dalloway' manuscript, showing Virginia Woolf's sketch of the proposed distribution of rooms at 52 Tavistock Square, on a page facing her draft text for the novel.

British Library, Additional MS 51044, folios 94 verso and 95

In November, Virginia's scheme - of writing her novel as well as reading for, and writing essays for, *The Common Reader* - caused her to turn to the back of the notebook in which she made notes for her essay on Greek literature. Here she recorded her thoughts on how she might develop her new novel. The specially bound plain paper notebooks in which she created her first drafts had wide margins in which she would scribble revisions and calculations. The blank left-hand page was also occasionally used for such notes, and one such page was put to a different use in the new year. For some time Virginia had been trying to persuade Leonard that they should return to Bloomsbury. Leonard resisted her pleas until the autumn of 1923, when Virginia began in earnest to look for a London home. Within three months she had found 52 Tavistock Square and bought a ten-year lease. During the following two months, she made plans for their move, using one of the blank pages of her *Mrs Dalloway/* 'The Hours' notebook to draw a rough plan of the allocation of rooms. The ground and first floors were tenanted by a firm of solicitors; in March the Hogarth Press was installed in the basement, where Virginia occupied a storeroom as her 'studio'.

In July, George (known as 'Dadie') Rylands became the latest recruit to the press. He stayed only until the end of the year, having successfully obtained a Cambridge fellowship, but he became a lasting friend. During his time at the press, Virginia's *Mr Bennett and Mrs Brown* was published in October - the month in which she finished writing *Mrs Dalloway* - and, in November, Volumes I and II of Freud's *Collected Papers* were also printed. In spring 1925, there was a trip to the south of France, before *The Common Reader* was published in April, and Virginia gave her Cambridge lecture on character in May, the month in which *Mrs Dalloway* was published. She had sent a proof copy of the novel to Jacques Raverat, an artist who had been one of the Neo-Pagans, and who was dying in France. Between 1922 and 1925, Virginia and Jacques had written to each other, often about their passion for their chosen arts of writing and painting. His wife, Gwen, had read the proof copy of *Mrs Dalloway* to Jacques, and before he died, in March 1925, he had dictated a letter to Virginia about the novel. Virginia wrote in her diary that his letter 'gave me one of the happiest days of my life. I wonder if this time I have achieved something? Well, nothing anyhow compared with Proust, in whom I am embedded now', for she was reading as voraciously as ever.

During the summer, the Woolfs visited friends and entertained for a frenzied three months. As Virginia's nephew, Quentin Bell, expressed it in his biography, 'There was bound to be a reckoning'. He recalled that in mid-August, at a Charleston party to celebrate his fifteenth birthday, quite suddenly, she:

> *rose, staggered, turned exactly the colour of a duck's egg and tried blindly and inefficiently to make her way out of the room. At that junction, when most of the company sat in stupid amazement, two persons acted promptly: Leonard and Vanessa moved swiftly and decisively, with the efficiency of long training, to do what was necessary - to take Virginia away from the room to fresh air, to a bed, and to administer whatever medicines experience had shown to be useful.*

Virginia with her nephew and later biographer, Quentin.

Dr Milo Keynes

The essay *On Being Ill* was the product of the period of ill health that followed this collapse, as was 'quick and flourishing work' on her next novel, *To the Lighthouse*, as well as a growing intimacy with Vita Sackville-West. Vita's husband, Harold Nicolson, was at the British Embassy in Tehran, Persia, and his wife was to join him early in 1926. Virginia's spirits were lowered by her feeble health, and the news that Vita would be leaving the country came as a blow. Ironically, at about the same time, news came of the death of Madge Vaughan, and Virginia failed to respond. In her diary, she observed, 'Madge died. Rustling among my emotions, I found nothing better than dead leaves. Her letters had eaten away the reality - the brilliancy, the warmth. Oh detestable time, that thus eats out the heart & lets the body go on.' Ironically, the next diary entry, over a week later, reads thus: 'I want to lie down like a tired child & weep away this life of care… Most children do not know what they cry for; nor do I altogether… Well, it is partly that devil Vita. No letter. No visit. No invitation to Long Barn. She was up last week, & never came… Only if I do not see her now, I shall not - ever: for the moment for intimacy will be gone, next summer.'

The 'moment for intimacy' came ten days later: encouraged by Leonard to write to Vita, and to accept her invitation, Virginia spent 17 and 18 December 1925 at Long Barn, Vita's home. These days have been described as the beginning of a love affair between the two women which lasted, despite Vita's interest in other women, a number of years. No one knows how they spent those first two days alone in December 1925. Each wrote about them afterwards. In a letter to Clive, Vita wrote, 'She came back here with me - more entrancing than ever', and went on to describe Virginia as 'incredibly lovely and fragile'. To her husband, Harold Nicolson, Vita wrote on 17 December, 1925:

> *I fetched V. and brought her down here [Long Barn]. She is an exquisite companion, and I love her dearly. Leonard is coming on Saturday. Please don't*
> *think   a) I shall fall in love with Virginia*
> *   b) Virginia will "   "   " me*
> *   c) Leonard   " " "   " "*
> *   d) I shall   " " "   " Leonard*
> *because it is not so.*

The following summer, she wrote to him:

You mention Virginia: it is simply laughable. I love Virginia - as who wouldn't? But really, my sweet, one's love for Virginia is a very different thing: a mental thing; a spiritual thing, if you like, an intellectual thing, and she inspires feelings of tenderness, which is, I suppose, owing to her funny mixture of hardness and softness - the hardness of her mind, and her terror of going mad again. She makes me feel protective. Also she loves me, which flatters and pleases me. Also - since I have embarked on telling you about Virginia - I am scared to death of arousing physical feelings in her, because of her madness. I don't know what effect it would have, you see: it is a fire with which I have no wish to play. I have too much real affection and respect for her... Virginia is not the sort of person one thinks of in that way. There is something incongruous and almost indecent in the idea. I have gone to bed with her (twice), but that's all.

In her diary, on 21 December 1925, Virginia wrote nothing so specific. She began by writing:

Leonard in Cassis, late 1920s.

Tate Gallery Archive

These Sapphists <u>love</u> women; friendship is never untinged with amorosity. In short, my fears and refrainings, my 'impertinence' my usual self-consciousness in intercourse with people who mayn't want me & so on - were all, as L. said, sheer fudge; &, partly thanks to him (he made me write) I wound up this wounded and stricken year in great style. I like her & being with her, & the splendour - she shines in the grocers shop in Sevenoaks with a candle lit radiance, stalking on legs like beech trees, pink glowing, grape clustered, pearl hung.

This was followed by comparisons with her own dowdiness and carelessness about her appearance 'Yet so beautiful, &c'. She asked herself, 'What is the effect of all this on me? Very mixed', and went on to make more comparisons, noting that Vita was, 'in short (what I have never been) a real woman.' Tellingly, she wrote that Vita 'so lavishes on me the maternal protection which, for some reason, is what I have always most wished from everyone. What L. gives me, & Nessa gives me, & Vita, in her more clumsy external way, tries to give me.' She finished the diary entry anticipating 'not without some trepidation' spending Christmas at Charleston, where there would be curiosity and, as it turned out, Clive's jealousy and Vanessa's 'none too merciful' treatment when Vita visited them all, the day after Christmas. Clive persisted in his desire to know if Vita and Virginia had slept together, questioning Vita at a New Year's party given by a friend, until Vita said, 'NEVER'.

Despite the lift to her spirits that the days with Vita had given, Virginia began 1926 still physically unwell, this time with German measles. During the spring, when Leonard reduced his hours of working at *The Nation and Athenaeum* to two days, and the British nation experienced the General Strike for ten days, Virginia managed to complete the first two of the three parts of *To the Lighthouse*. Building improvements - specifically, running hot water and flushing lavatories - had been made to Monk's House, and so they spent four days there at the end of May. In June, Vita stayed at Monk's House with Virginia after returning from Persia. The visit was part of a summer in which socializing was periodically interrupted by Virginia's uncertain health, and her writing of a number of articles, as well as the novel.

The Woolfs stayed at Ottoline Morrell's home at Garsington during a weekend in June when Aldous Huxley and Siegfried Sassoon were also visiting. Virginia met and got on with H.G. Wells, and with Leonard visited both Robert Bridges and Thomas Hardy. The latter, aged 85, Virginia described in her diary as 'a little puffy cheeked cheerful old man, with an atmosphere cheerful & businesslike in addressing us, rather like an old doctor's or solicitor's, saying "Well now -" or words like that as he shook hands.' Virginia's father had been Editor of the *Cornhill Magazine*, and had published *Far From the Madding Crowd* in serial form. Hardy talked a little about the effects of writing for a magazine which needed a dramatic conclusion to each serialized section: 'I daresay *F. from the M.C.* would have been a great deal better if I had written it differently', Virginia reported his saying, commenting herself, 'The truth is he is a very kind man'.

Within days of this visit, Virginia experienced what she described in her diary as 'a whole nervous breakdown in miniature'. She felt an 'enormous desire for rest' and withdrew from society to Monk's House for two or three months, during which she felt 'intense depression' and wrote about her state of mind:

> *Woke up perhaps at 3. Oh its beginning its coming - the horror - physically like a painful wave swelling about the heart - tossing me up. I'm unhappy, unhappy! Down - God, I wish I were dead. Pause. But why am I feeling this? Let me watch the wave rise. I watch. Vanessa. Children. Failure. Yes; I detect that. Failure failure. (The wave rises). Oh they laughed at my taste in green paint! Wave crashes. I wish I were dead! I've only a few years to live I hope. I cant face this horror any more - (this is the wave spreading out over me).*

> *This goes on; several times, with varieties of horror. Then, at the crisis, instead of the pain remaining intense, it becomes rather vague. I doze. I wake with a start. The wave again! The irrational pain: the sense of failure... Does everyone go through this state? Why have I so little control? It is not creditable, nor lovable. It is the cause of much waste & pain in my life.*

Virginia with short hair, by a fireplace with tiles decorated by Vanessa and Duncan Grant, and sitting on a chair upholstered in a fabric designed by them.

Random House, London

Hyde Park Gate News.

VOL II. NO 35   September. Monday 12th 1892.

Mr Thoby Stephen's birthday was on last Thursday. It was of course raining all day except during 2 or 3 hours in the evening. Mrs Stephen gave Mr Thoby a very handsome box to contain his butterflies and moths. Mr Gerald Duckworth always gives him a splendid display of fireworks in the evening. Mrs Hunt accompanied by her little family and those who are staying with her came up early in the afternoon and played games until tea-time. They played the exciting game of "Cat and Mouse" and even Mr Headlam was made to join. He caused great amusement by sitting down in a chair when he was mouse and allowing Miss Stillman who was cat to run round and round after him thinking that the juveniles were laughing at her for not catching him. Mrs Stephen tried to guide her towards him but she seemed to have an instinct which would not let her touch him. Uproarius laughter continued during the whole scene. Thus passed the afternoon. Tea was soon announced and the whole party trooped merrily into the dining-room. Near the end of the tea Mr Thoby Stephen cut his cake but in such big slices that Mrs Stephen thought it advisable to take the knife. Miss Stillman got up some charades after tea which were most amusing and were heartily applauded especially the scene where Mr Gerald Duckworth poked Mr Hills with a javelin. Already the cries of th children upon the lawn were making themselves heard when the charades ended. The children were super-exuberant and were kept back with great difficulty and Mrs Stephen was made rightly indignant by the bigger and elder children pushing back the smaller ones so that they could not see the fireworks. The balloon went up first and they were pronounced a success as only the first one burnt and the others actually went right out of sight! The rest of the fireworks went off rippingly but the garden next day was a scene of ruin and destruction. The gate was entirely broken off its hinges but that was not so very wonderful as it had never been extraordinary for its strength

On Saturday morning Master Hilary Hunt and Master Basil Smith came up to Talland House and asked Master Thoby and Miss Virginia Stephen to accompany them to the light-house as Freeman the boatman

The Hyde Park Gate News *for 12 September 1892, which gives an account - starting in the fourth column - of a trip to the lighthouse and descibes Adrian's disappointment at being left at home*

British Library, Additional MS 70725, folios 71 to 72 verso

The day after this diary entry, on 16 September 1926, she 'finished, provisionally' *To the Lighthouse*.

In the autumn of 1926, after her 'season of profound despondency', Virginia revised the text of *To the Lighthouse* which was published, on the anniversary of her mother's death, on 5 May 1927. By this time, she had experienced 'the most important event in my life since marriage - so Clive described it': she had had her hair cut, or 'shingled' in February, and decided to be 'short haired for life'. Whilst said that there was a perfect tide and wind for going there. Master Adrian Stephen was much disappointed at not being allowed to go. On arriving at the light-house Miss Virginia Stephen saw a small and dilapidated bird standing on one leg on the light-house. Mrs Hunt called the man and asked him how it had got there. He said that it had been blown there and they then saw that it had been ~~blown~~ ~~there~~ picked out. On the way home Master Basil Smith "spued like fury".

A COCKNEY'S FARMING EXPERIENCES.

CHAPTER IV.

Next morning I determined to be as agreeable as I could to Harriet as I did not think it proper for two young people to be always falling out as we had done. I went down stairs with the coat she liked best on and did not make any personal remarks about her and did not take my dog into the drawing room. I ventured further on in the day to ask Harriet by what name the dog should be called and she replied quite amiably "Oh call him Lick because he licked my face. I did not think it a very nice name

72

but assented remembering my resolution of the morning. As I had no horses I determined to buy one but remembering my experience with the dog I resolved to have an experienced horse-dealer with me. Thanks to him I bought a very fine cart-horse. I fastened the horse to the garden roller and rolled up and down the lawn quite nicely as I thought. But after an hour when I found that I wasn't getting on I thought that there must be some quicker way of progressing I therefore brought out my best walking-stick which was an ebony one with a silver handle with a gold plate with

my name and address inscribed on it. With this I pushed violently against the roller for some time until a large crack caused me to shudder and a portion of the stick flew to a distance of 6 yards. I got thoroughly disgusted and ran away heedless of the horse who stood quietly browsing the grass. But as I was going I was suddenly called back by the clattering of hoofs, the rolling of the roller and the yelping of a dog. I turned back and saw my dear Lick being kicked unmercifully by the strong legs of my gallant carthorse. I rescued Lick finding that he had received no injury worth speaking of. I soon went to bed tired by the fatiguing day.

waiting for her novel to appear, Virginia concentrated on articles and reviews, as well as travel. Duncan Grant had been taken ill whilst visiting his mother and aunt in Cassis, in the South of France at the beginning of the year. Vanessa had rushed off with their daughter, Angelica, to find him almost recovered. They all remained there, where the light was perfect for painting, and were joined by Clive, who was recovering from his love affair with Mary Hutchinson. The Woolfs spent a week with them at the beginning of April before travelling to Italy, which Virginia loved, and where she caught sight of D.H. Lawrence through a railway carriage window. They were away for almost a month, returning the week before *To the Lighthouse* was published.

Virginia sent copies of the novel to Vanessa and Duncan. When she could bear their silence no longer, she wrote a letter to her sister in the form of a play-scene. It featured an imagined conversation between Vanessa and Duncan concerning their disinclination to read the novel, and their dread at having to tell Virginia what they thought of it. This letter crossed with one from Vanessa:

> *it seemed to me in the first part of the book you have given a portrait of mother which is more like her to me than anything I could ever have conceived of as possible. It is almost painful to have her so raised from the dead. You have made one feel the extraordinary beauty of her character, which must be the most difficult thing in the world to do. It was like meeting her again with oneself grown up & on equal terms & it seems to me the most astonishing feat of creation to have been able to see her in such a way - You have given father too I think as clearly... So you see as far as portrait painting goes you seem to me to be a supreme artist... In fact for the last two days I have hardly been able to attend to daily life... I wonder how Adrian will like James!*

Inevitably, the resemblance of the novel's Mr and Mrs Ramsay and their son, James, to Leslie and Julia Stephen and their younger son, Adrian, were the aspects of the novel that struck and affected Vanessa. Although the setting of the novel was the Hebrides, it was clear to Vanessa that the novel evoked their childhood in St Ives. The Ramsays, like the Stephens, have eight children and, like Leslie Stephen, Mr Ramsay in the novel has invited an assortment of friends to spend the summer with his family at their seaside home. The *Hyde Park Gate News* had recorded Adrian's disappointment in not going to the lighthouse, an event that Vanessa recalled when reading the novel. But *To the Lighthouse* was more to Virginia than an evocation of childhood. One critic summed it up as 'a statement about time and death and the permanence of art', and it was with art and artistry that Virginia was concerned as much as she was with having 'father's character done complete in it'. Lily Briscoe struggles to convey her meaning through art, and completes in the third part of the novel, the painting she had begun in the first. Her last brush stroke marks the end of the novel:

> *It was done; it was finished. Yes, she thought, laying down her brush in extreme fatigue, I have had my vision.*

It was in writing this novel that Virginia had expressed the feeling that 'novel' was an inadequate word for what she was trying to write: 'I have an idea that I will invent a new name for my books to supplant 'novel'. A new --- by Virginia Woolf. But what? Elegy?'. Leonard and Clive both thought it a 'masterpiece', and even Arnold Bennett, her old adversary, conceded in a review that 'It is the best book of hers that I know. Her character drawing has improved.'

Godrevy Lighthouse, St Ives, which can still be seen from Talland House.

William Heller, Digital Imagemakers, St Ives

➤ *Feminine Identities*

Just as income from the publication of *Mrs Dalloway* had brought flushing lavatories to Monk's House, so the success of *To the Lighthouse* enabled the Woolfs to acquire a car. Although Virginia took driving lessons and initially enjoyed taking charge at the wheel, a number of accidents persuaded her that she much preferred being a passenger. Vita was a much more competent motorist. She and her husband and the Woolfs saw each other a number of times during the summer of 1927, once to witness the total eclipse of the sun. This was also the summer in which Virginia and Leonard gave a joint radio talk, alas not recorded, in which she opined that books 'should be as cheap and easy to purchase as a packet of cigarettes'. She was again reading voraciously, and wrote on the subject of biography, praising Harold Nicolson for his 'lack of pose, humbug, solemnity' in writing about great men and institutions. A late summer visit to Vita and Harold Nicolson's home led Virginia to combine thoughts of biography, Vita and fiction into her next novel, *Orlando*. The Woolfs visited Long Barn in September, where Vita had dressed her son, Nigel, as a Russian boy. Virginia recorded in her diary that he had protested, 'Dont. It makes me look like a little girl'. In the same diary entry she noted that, in bed, the night following the visit, she contemplated producing 'a grand historical picture… The question is how to do it. Vita should be Orlando, a young nobleman' - and so she became. Within two weeks, the idea had formulated into a clear plan: 'a biography beginning in the year 1500 & continuing to the present day, called Orlando: Vita; only with a change about from one sex to another.'

MR. HUGH WALPOLE making the formal presentation of the *Femina-Vie Heureuse* prize to Mrs. Virginia Woolf.

Apart from writing about the novels of E.M. Forster, Virginia enthusiastically devoted most of her energies to writing

Orlando in the latter months of 1927. Early in 1928, Thomas Hardy died. The news of his death threw a gloomy pall over the start of the year. The novel, having begun as a joke, turned sour and long-winded, refusing to be finished until late-March. Having told Vita she was 'sick of it' before leaving to spend a month with Vanessa and her entourage, once again in Cassis, Virginia did not revise her view when she re-read the completed novel upon her return. Being awarded the £40 *Prix Femina Vie Heureuse* for *To the Lighthouse* provided no consolation; she thought it the 'most insignificant and ridiculous of prizes' and felt that she had 'looked ugly in cheap black clothes' at the award ceremony. The only positive outcome was that the prize was presented to her by the author Hugh Walpole, who became a friend.

As yet another young man, Angus Davidson, departed from the Hogarth Press, Leonard took on a 16-year-old, Richard Kennedy, early in 1928. Kennedy was to write hilariously, in mock-diary form more than forty years later, of his time as *A Boy at the Hogarth Press*. In an entry dated 30 June 1928 and headed 'Mrs W at Work' he described the press's basement storeroom at Tavistock Square in which Virginia wrote most mornings, surrounded by parcels of books:

Virginia Woolf writing in the packing room at Tavistock Square, by Richard Kennedy, from his A Boy at the Hogarth Press.

Courtesy of Mrs Olive Kennedy

> *Sitting in her little space by the gas fire, she reminds me of the Bruce Bairnsfather veterans of the War, surrounded by sandbags. She looks at us over the top of her steel-rimmed spectacles, her grey hair hanging over her forehead and a shag cigarette hanging from her lips. She wears a hatchet-blue overall and sits hunched in a wicker arm-chair with her pad on her knees and a small typewriter beside her.*

Later that summer Richard Kennedy was a visitor to Monk's House, as were several others, including E.M. Forster and Vita. Somewhat to Leonard's irritation,

Virginia and Vita planned a week's holiday in France, which they took at the end of September. Virginia wrote daily to Leonard and when, on the fourth day, Vita had heard from Harold but Virginia had received no letter from Leonard, she sent a postcard, a letter and then a telegram. His letter arrived the next day. It included news of family and friends, and a message Virginia had longed to receive: 'It is very dreary without you… I hope you wont make a habit of deserting me.' In her reply to him, written on the same day, Virginia looked forward to being home: 'I think we shall have a very happy and exciting autumn, in spite of the complete failure of Orlando.'

Since early in the year, Virginia had been thinking about 'Women and Fiction', the subject upon which she had been invited to speak at Cambridge. Her relationship with Vita, writing *Orlando* - which she dedicated to Vita - and publishing what she described to Vita as 'a nice little story about Sapphism, for the Americans' all contributed to making her willing, upon her return from France, to testify in a court case brought against the publication of Radclyffe Hall's *The Well of Loneliness*. The novel's sympathetic depiction of lesbian love contravened the existing obscenity laws and it was banned. Leonard had been at the forefront of public protest at its proposed banning although, like many writers who supported him, he thought little of its literary qualities. The timing of the prosecution case, the week before *Orlando* was published, could not have been better calculated to ensure that Virginia's latest novel was anything but the failure she had predicted. And, as Leonard wrote in his autobiography, 'After 1928 we were always very well off. In the next ten years our income was anything from twice to six times what it had been in 1924… and we did more of the things we wanted to do, for instance travel, and less in the occupations which we did not want to do, for instance journalism.'

The Woolfs' first journey after the publication of *Orlando* was only as far as Cambridge, accompanied by Vanessa and Angelica, where Virginia read her paper on 'Women and Fiction' to the Arts Society. Virginia and Leonard stayed with Pernel Strachey, who was Principal of Newnham College - then, as now, a women's college - and had lunch the next day at King's College, Cambridge. A week later, Virginia returned to Cambridge, this time with Vita, to speak at the second women's college, Girton - to the students' ODTAA (One Damn Thing After Another) Society. The talks were to be revised and expanded to become the essay, *A Room of One's Own*.

The sort of travel to which Leonard had referred was undertaken at the beginning of 1929, after the third edition of *Orlando* had been ordered. They visited Berlin, where Harold Nicolson held a diplomatic post, and were joined by Vanessa, Duncan and Quentin. Eschewing the luncheons arranged by Harold, and the cabaret-life described by Christopher Isherwood in *I am a Camera*, their lives were, as Vanessa expressed it in a letter to her other son, Julian, 'enlivened by a certain amount of human drama. The Nicolsons play a large part in the Woolves' existence.

Leonard and Virginia with their Singer motor car in Cassis.

Tate Gallery Archive

Virginia Woolf

Vita is in a state of rage and despair. She hates the Germans, who won't let her take her dog for a walk freely, drive in her car without passing 3 medical exams or do any of the things she likes.' All in all, the short trip was not a success. On the return journey, Virginia took a tablet to prevent sea-sickness, and experienced a violent adverse reaction which made her ill and incapable of socializing for six weeks. This period of quiet gave her an opportunity to revise her Cambridge lectures and produce *A Room of One's Own*, the core idea of which is expressed in 'the prosaic conclusion - that it is necessary to have five hundred a year and a room with a lock on the door if you are to write fiction or poetry.'

Ever since the summer of 1927, when Vanessa had written to Virginia about 'a huge moth - half a foot, literally, across' which they let into their house in Cassis, Virginia had been contemplating a new fictional piece. In March 1929 she wrote to her nephew, Quentin, that she was 'thinking about a book which I shall call the Moths I think - an entirely new kind of book. But it will never be so good as it is now in my mind unwritten'. The moths would eventually become *The Waves*, but meanwhile she was using her imagination for quite other practical purposes: an extension was to be built onto Monk's House. In her diary, Virginia wrote, 'I am summoning Philcox next week to plan a room - I have money to build it, money to furnish it.' Earlier in the same diary entry, she had written:

> *Old age is withering us... Only in myself, I say, forever bubbles this impetuous torrent. So that even if I see ugliness in the glass, I think, very well, inwardly I am more full of shape & colour than ever. I think I am bolder as a writer. I am alarmed by my own cruelty with my friends. Clive, I say, is intolerably dull. Francis is a runaway milk lorry.*

Francis Birrell was an old Bloomsbury friend who had a year or two earlier been considered as a potential Hogarth Press partner, and who was, like Virginia and Clive, also 'all wrinkled and dusty' in Virginia's opinion. A year later, Cecil Beaton was to describe Virginia as:

> *one of the most gravely distinguished-looking women I have ever seen... Her fine skin is parchment-coloured, she has timid startled eyes, set deep, a sharp bird-like nose and firm pursed lips. Her lank hair and aristocratic wrists are of a supreme delicacy... She wears cameo brooches and cotton gloves, and hatpins, and exudes an atmosphere of musk and old lace... but her old-fashioned dowdinesses are but a conscious and literary game of pretence, for she is alertly contemporary, even a little ahead of her time. Many of her confreres see her as a Juno, awe-inspiring and gaunt, but she herself is frightened, a bundle of tentative gestures, and quick nervous glances, as frail and crisp as a dead leaf; and like a sea-anemone she curls up at contact with the outer world.*

Virginia was much preoccupied at this time with the notion of 'self' or 'selves'. She had written of Orlando that 'she had a great variety of selves to call upon'. In *The Waves*, the private and public selves of the six principal characters, or perhaps the selves of one character, would be evoked through interior monologues - sometimes

85

Virginia 'talking through her hat' at Ray Strachey's Mud House.

The Lilly Library, Indiana University, Bloomington, Indiana

described as and confused with the stream of consciousness technique - set against the rising and setting of the sun, and the constant movement of the waves.

Alongside her musings for the moths novel, Virginia had been struggling to complete *Phases of Fiction*, the product of her reading. As Leonard noted in his autobiography, after the publication of *Orlando* they each produced less journalism and, in the summer of 1929, they invited fewer people to stay at Monk's House. At the end of May, they were there in order to vote in the General Election, which resulted in the second Labour government. They spent ten days in Cassis in June but were otherwise mostly at Monk's House, where Virginia's recurrent headaches were accompanied by low spirits. Nevertheless, she continued to write 'Waves or Moths or whatever it is to be called. One thinks one has learnt to write quickly; & one hasn't. And what is odd, I'm not writing with gusto or pleasure because of the concentration. I am not reeling it off; but sticking it down.'

A Room of One's Own was published in October and sold well. At Tavistock Square, noise from a nearby hotel drove them to take legal action, so that the completion of Virginia's new Monk's House bedroom at the end of the year was most welcome. Virginia managed to avoid her accustomed start-of-the year illness until February, by which time she had met, and failed to be impressed by, Ramsay MacDonald, the Prime Minister. A more lasting and positive impression was to be left by the composer, Ethel Smyth, who 'bounced' into Virginia's life a month later.

Virginia still had a high temperature and was being advised to rest when Ethel arrived for tea and, as Virginia wrote in her diary on 21 February 1930, 'the basis of an undying friendship (was) made in 15 minutes'. She was 72 years old and would outlive Virginia. Having written the suffragette's anthem and served two months in prison when fighting for votes for women in 1911, Ethel had, in later life, got to know Ottoline Morrell, read *A Room of One's Own* and resolved to meet Virginia. They were to become close friends, Ethel adoring Virginia, visiting frequently and sometimes writing her two letters a day.

Throughout the spring, during which Leonard finally left *The Nation*, Virginia wrote and completed a first draft of *The Waves*. She and Leonard spent a good deal of time at Monk's House in the spring and summer,

Dame Ethel Smyth, composer, suffragette in her 50s and, in her 70s and 80s 'undying friend' of Virginia.

Random House, London

sometimes with visitors, sometimes alone, Virginia revising her novel. At the end of August, Virginia experienced what she described as her 'brush with death':

> *I was walking down the path with Lydia. If this dont stop, I said, referring to the bitter taste in my mouth & the pressure like a wire cage of sound over my head, then I am ill: yes, very likely I am destroyed, diseased, dead. Damn it! Here I fell down - saying 'How strange - flowers'. In scraps I felt & knew myself carried into the sitting room by Maynard, saw L. look very frightened; said I will go upstairs; the drumming of my heart, the pain, the effort got violent at the doorstep; overcame me; like gas; I was unconscious; then the wall & the picture returned to my eyes; I saw life again. Strange I said, & so lay, gradually recovering till 11 when I crept up to bed. Today, Tuesday, I am in the lodge & Ethel comes - valiant old woman!*

Maynard Keynes and his Russian ballet dancer wife, Lydia Lopokova. Lydia was observed by Virginia as a potential model for Rezia in Mrs Dalloway

Dr Milo Keynes

This fainting fit, the symptoms of which anyone who suffers from low blood-pressure will readily recognize, was followed by ten days of feeling unwell, with 'the usual - oh how usual - headache', but in less than two weeks the Woolfs were able to visit Vita's new home, Sissinghurst Castle, where, once a new press had been purchased, they deposited the original one. They even managed lunch with Vanessa and family at Charleston, with George Duckworth and his wife. Slowly, with the interruptions of socializing, Virginia worked towards finishing her novel, through the autumn and up to Christmas when, earlier than usual, her winter bout of influenza arrived, delaying its completion.

A new distraction came at the beginning of 1931. Pippa Strachey invited Virginia to speak to the London and National Society for Women's Service on 21 January. In her talk, 'Professions for Women' was the germ of an idea that was in several years' time to become two works, *The Years* and *Three Guineas*. She told the 'well dressed, keen, & often beautiful young women' whom she addressed:

> *I discovered that if I were going to review books I should need to do battle with a certain phantom. And the phantom was a woman... The Angel in the House... It was she who bothered me and wasted my time and so tormented me that at last I killed her... I will describe her as shortly as I can. She was intensely sympathetic. She was immensely charming. She was utterly unselfish. She excelled in the difficult arts of family life. She sacrificed herself daily. If there was a chicken, she took the leg; if there was a draught she sat in it... Above all - I need not say it - she was pure.*

In short, she was Julia Stephen, mother of Virginia Woolf. If writing *To the Lighthouse* had not laid Julia's ghost, this talk and the works that developed from it would expose and put an end to all the restricting values that her mother had embodied.

A day or two after she gave the talk, Virginia's temperature had risen and her headaches had returned. On 25 January 1931, however, she celebrated her forty-ninth birthday, noting in her diary that she had 'returned to Waves... seen the entire book whole' and thought she could finish it in less than three weeks. In fact, it was on 7 February that she did so, thus laying another family ghost:

> *Anyhow, it is done; & I have been sitting these 15 minutes in a state of glory, & calm, & some tears, thinking of Thoby & if I could write Julian Thoby Stephen 1881-1906 on the first page. I suppose not. How physical the sense of triumph & relief is! Whether good or bad, its done; & as I certainly felt at the end, not merely finished, but rounded off, completed, the thing stated.*

The Hogarth Press, under the new management of John Lehmann, a friend of Virginia's nephew, Julian Bell, would publish the novel in October; it outsold all her earlier works. Having finished her own work of art, she turned her mind to music and pictures, specifically Purcell's *Faery Queen*, Ethel's choral symphony, *The Prison*, and Roger Fry's show of forty years' work. Roger had visited them, embittered and morose, just before Christmas and, after she visited the exhibition of his work in February, she wrote him a delicious letter. Nearer the end of her life, in 1940, she would write a similarly loving letter to George Bernard Shaw. In her letter to Roger in 1931, however she wrote, 'I am going to lay my tribute at your feet', and went on to comment on the beauty of his pictures, and to express her 'deep admiration (of) the perpetual adventure of your mind'. She congratulated him on his 'striding ahead, never giving up or lying down and becoming inert and torpid and commonplace like other people', and invited him and Helen Anrep, with whom he had lived since 1926, to dinner.

In the summer of 1931, art intruded on Virginia's life in a way she had never anticipated. Never having liked being looked at, drawn, photographed or painted, Virginia agreed to Stephen Tomlin's making a sculpture of her head. This meant she would have to undergo even closer inspection than any of the other processes would have involved. She loathed the experience and sat as few times as possible during July and August, a period of political and financial crisis in Britain and the United States. Although much involved in politics, Leonard spent two days in July reading the typescript of *The Waves* and, after walking out to Virginia's writing lodge in the

Leonard and Virginia in the garden at Monk's House.

Random House, London

garden at Monk's House, told her, 'It is a masterpiece'. Greater praise, she felt, she could not have received, but she was already undertaking a more light-hearted writing project. It was to be another mock-biography, this time of a dog. In reading the letters of Elizabeth Barrett and Robert Browning, Virginia had been amused by Miss Barrett's pet spaniel, Flush - 'so I couldn't resist making him a life'. Virginia's own dog, Pinka (sometimes 'Pinker') was also a spaniel, much beloved by both Leonard and Virginia. Pinka's photograph appeared as the frontispiece of the first edition.

Virginia and Leonard had spent two weeks in France in the spring, and they agreed that they would now spend more time at Monk's House. Headaches plagued her on and off during the summer but, more than anything, life at Monk's House replenished her spirit. She was able to write in September, 'the last few days have been heavenly... how sweet life is with L. here, in its regularity & order, & the garden & the room at night & music & my walks & writing easily & interestedly'. The reviews of *The Waves* in October, when they had returned to London, were generally good. It was the *Times Literary Supplement* half-column review of Leonard's *After the Deluge* that 'damped and disheartened' her. His despondency was reminiscent of her father's gloom in old age, and it infected the atmosphere of home. Although better reviews, sales and the excitement of another General Election lightened the atmosphere, Virginia's headaches returned in November. Morgan Forster wrote a letter praising *The Waves* that gave her great pleasure, as did one from an old friend, Goldsworthy Lowes Dickinson. To him she wrote that in the novel she had meant that

> *in some vague way we are the same person, and not separate people. The six characters were supposed to be one. I'm getting old myself - I shall be fifty next year; and I come to feel more and more how difficult it is to collect oneself into one Virginia.*

Once again, the headaches caused her to withdraw from society, this time for a month. Towards the end of that month, she dreamt of being in fits of laughter with Lytton at the theatre, and so she wrote him a letter. She had no idea that he was seriously ill with stomach cancer.

≈ *Friends Depart*

On Christmas morning 1931, Virginia began her diary with the words, 'Lytton is still alive this morning.' In each of her diary entries thereafter she noted his state of health. She and Leonard drove to his home on 14 January 1932, but he was too ill to see them. On 22 January 1932, she wrote in her diary: 'Lytton died yesterday morning'. Although she had not seen him often, and had not admired his later work, she still thought of Lytton as a dear friend. His brother Oliver, who had married Virginia's Neo-Pagan friend, Ray Costelloe in 1911, dined with the Woolfs just over a week after Lytton's death, and they discussed Carrington's wish to kill herself. There was little Virginia could do, and so she focused on writing non-fiction. When Carrington's husband, Ralph Partridge, asked Virginia and Leonard to visit his wife, they did. It was only when Carrington took Virginia to Lytton's room that she sobbed in Virginia's arms, saying she had 'always been a failure'. They left, and the next day Carrington shot herself.

Such events provided a grim start to the year of Virginia's fiftieth birthday and the Woolfs' twentieth wedding anniversary. Virginia and Leonard agreed at the end of one of their 'mausoleum talks', as Leonard called them, that they needed to plan for happier events 'after this morbid time'. Consequently, after spending a sociable Easter, they travelled for four weeks with Roger Fry and his sister, Margery, to Paris, Venice, Athens and Belgrade, returning on the Orient Express. Inevitably the journey recalled that taken shortly before Thoby's death, and Virginia could not shake off feelings of depression for some time after. Social life continued, including a lunch in June with Shaw, recorded in her diary, and Virginia finished *The Common Reader: Second Series*. In August, news came of Goldsworthy Lowes Dickinson's sudden and unexpected death, bringing on more mausoleum talk and thought.

The weather became very hot, and Virginia experienced another fainting fit. This time she was quick to recover, resuming her writing and their social life, and attending the Labour Party Conference in October. The same month, even though she had not finished writing *Flush*, she began writing what she provisionally called 'The Pargiters', the novel-essay that would become *The Years*, in which she intended to sum up her life and times. Being busy with her own writing, Virginia affected not to read Winifred Holtby's biography of her. She told Ethel it had greatly amused her when she had dipped into it. She had not resisted Holtby's request as much as might be expected, often being helpful to the young writer. In fact, she was more agitated by the photograph of her chosen for the frontispiece than by anything Holtby wrote. In the two months just before Christmas she calculated her own writing as amounting to 60,320 words. A few days later, she was despairing that 'the 30,000 words of Flush... won't do'. But at the end of the year she concluded that the autumn had been 'a great season of liberation' and resolved that she would not allow her feelings of exhilaration to be obliterated by 'the usual black despair'. She would savour the joys of the present.

Family group at Charleston, 1930. Standing are Leonard with Pinka (or 'Pinker') the model for Flush, Clive, Julian, Virginia, Auberon Duckworth and Duncan Grant; Quentin is in front.

Tate Gallery Archive

At the beginning of 1933 Virginia's health was strong and she quickly settled to correcting *Flush*. She was also absorbed in writing 'The Pargiters', which had had its origins in her talk on 'The Angel in the House'. In the persona of Elvira Pargiter, Virginia had just expressed the view that society was corrupt and women should 'take nothing that it can give' when, in March, Manchester University offered her an honorary doctorate. Virginia refused it, as she had the previous year refused Cambridge University's invitation to deliver the Clark Lectures, and its offer of the

Leslie Stephen lectureship in September 1933. Her intention in 'The Pargiters' was to make it clear why such seductions of the establishment should be resisted. The work was a new experiment in form, expressing the ideas of the lecture hall in both fiction and essay. Achieving that end was to prove impossible. Writing and rewriting was to take much of her time and sap much of her energy over the next four to five years, and she ultimately published two works. The long essay or polemic, *Three Guineas*, made clear why university honours such as those offered to her should be refused. In April, a meeting with Bruno Walter - the conductor who had recently been forced to leave Germany because of his opposition to Hitler - intensified her resolve. A chance meeting with Shaw provided an amusing distraction.

Virginia had been taking Italian lessons twice a week for several months in preparation for a holiday in Italy, where she and Leonard drove and spent most of May 1933. After they returned, her life was consumed for two months or so by writing and socializing in London and Sussex. The result was exhaustion and bed-rest in August. Nevertheless, once she was again well, she kept the promise she had made to herself after Lytton's death - that she would be sure not to lose contact with old friends - and attended a meeting of the revised Memoir Club. She had E.M. Forster to stay and several friends to tea at Monk's House. There was the annual Labour Party Conference to attend and, on the day *Flush* was published, a visit to Sissinghurst. The socializing continued up to and including Christmas.

The year of 1934 began with the death and funeral of Leonard's sister, Clara. As Virginia had always remained aloof from Leonard's family, dutifully seeing her mother-in-law from time to time, but otherwise having little other contact, the death had little impact. Closer to home, quite literally, was another emotional wrench: her cook, Nelly Boxall, had become intolerable and would have to be dismissed. Virginia finally summoned up the courage in March: 'I feel executioner & the executed in one,' she wrote on the eve of Nelly's going, but on the day itself - 'Lord what a relief now!' It was also a relief to be rid of six weeks of headaches.

The spring signalled another trip abroad, this time to Ireland. After visiting and staying a night at the home of the writer Elizabeth Bowen, they continued with their motor tour, but they had been in the country less than a week when they read in *The Times* of George Duckworth's death.

I feel the usual incongruous shades of feeling... But I remember the genuine glow, from last summer when I went to see him... how childhood goes with him - the batting, the laughter, the treats... that was the best which oddly enough returned of late years a little.

They went on with their holiday, enjoying the country but growing tired of hotels. Within days of returning, Virginia was in bed with influenza, which lingered on until the end of May. She then focused her attention on 'The Pargiters'; Leonard focused his on a new pet - a marmoset called Mitzi, which delighted in sitting on his head. At Monk's House in August much of the talk with friends was of political and economic disaster in Britain, Europe and America. Her nephew, Julian, was at an anti-war demonstration in London on 9 September when news reached his mother and aunt in Sussex that Roger Fry had died. The impact of the news was tremendous and lasting Roger and Virginia had kept up for many years an intermittent conversation about art and literature that had influenced and altered the work of each. He was more than a friend, as Lytton had been; he was part of her very thought processes. Not long after the funeral, Roger's sister Margery asked Virginia to write his biography. Initially, she was reluctant, but eventually she took on the task.

George and Lady Margaret Duckworth at Charleston, 1930. This picture might well be borne in mind when reading of Hugh and Evelyn Whitbread in Virginia's novel, Mrs Dalloway.

Tate Gallery Archive

But before that, she wished to finish 'The Pargiters'. That autumn and winter - during which the criticism of her work by Wyndham Lewis, a writer and experimental artist who had right-wing political leanings, lowered her spirits considerably - Virginia finished her first draft and began rewriting. Her system of a decade before, of writing journalism, fiction, and her diary, had practically ceased. In 1933 she had published only one review and one article; in 1934 she wrote a couple more. Whatever her current output, she was a famous writer and, as such, in November she was photographed by Man Ray. At the end of the year, as a break from the novel, she worked again on an old project, *Freshwater*, a farcical play for her family's entertainment at Angelica's birthday party.

On 2 January 1935, Francis Birrell, whom Virginia had described in her diary in 1929 as 'a runaway milk lorry', died. Now she wrote, 'It was a mercy, as we say, that it ended so soon. But a queer thing, death. Last night I suddenly thought, how silly & indeed disgusting death, the decomposition of the body, &c. Why think of it

as anything noble?'. She and Leonard 'talked about Francis' with Maynard and Lydia Keynes, after which Maynard 'read us a long magnificently spry and juicy letter from Shaw, on a sickbed, aged 77'. Shaw's health recovered; her own life went on, and the performance of *Freshwater* later in the month was 'an unbuttoned laughing evening'. Much socializing in Tavistock Square and at Monk's House was combined with revising 'The Pargiters'. She realized, in the spring, that 'this fiction is dangerously near propaganda' and decided to steer clear of the feminist essay with which she had intended to combine the Pargiters' story, and which she now referred to as 'On Being Despised, or whatever it is to be called'.

In May, taking Mitzi the marmoset with them, the Woolfs toured Holland, Germany - where they saw a banner declaring 'The Jew is our enemy' - Italy and France, meeting Vanessa, Quentin and Angelica in Rome. When they returned home, Pinka had just died. This depressed both of them, and they found life without their spaniel difficult, taking some consolation in acquiring another, called

Sally, at the end of June. In July, Virginia opened an exhibition of Roger Fry's work in Bristol. There was the usual socializing in the summer, interrupted by a surprise when Vanessa's son Julian announced that he had been offered the post of Professor of English at the University of Wuhan in China, and left at the end of August.

A few days later, in the margin of her diary, next to a note about a new umbrella, Virginia wrote, 'And I think I will call the book 'The Years'. Giving her novel a title made it no easier to write, however, especially when she wanted to start on the biography of Roger Fry. In the autumn and winter, there were other distractions, many of a political sort, and another General Election - which was won by the Conservatives - in November. Leonard was much involved in canvassing for the Labour party in Sussex, and Virginia joked about calling on Vita's aristocratic mother for tea, speculating that the next day's newspaper placards would declare 'Lady Novelist poisoned by Peeress'. In December, she had her palm read.

The lady novelist was dragging on, retyping 'the impossible eternal book', *The Years*, and preparing Roger's biography at the beginning of January, 1936, the first few days of which were blighted by a severe headache. Virginia was unwell and had to rest in bed from time to time throughout the year. The Hogarth Press had not done well during the previous year, Virginia had failed to earn enough to cover her share of the Woolfs' joint expenditure, and political events were not calculated to lift the mood. King George died in January and was succeeded by Edward VIII, who had right-wing sympathies, and would abdicate at the end of the year. Fascist and anti-fascist meetings were held, one of the latter at Virginia's brother Adrian's home in February. The same month, Vita's mother died. The following month Hitler invaded the Rhineland, and Virginia was suffering 'acute despair on re-reading' *The Years*, which she felt was a 'failure'. For two months in April and May, and four months from June to October, she wrote no diary entries. Her menopause had begun - 'the swollen veins - the tingling; the odd falling; feeling of despair. Brain not fully blooded. Hot & cold' - and all the old symptoms of headaches, sleeplessness, faintness, distress and so on, simply wore her down. She felt suicidal in a way she had not felt since the year after her marriage, in 1913.

Thanks to Leonard's acting skills ('He was in tears'), Virginia's misery lifted completely in November when he told her he liked *The Years* better than *The Waves*.

Opposite:

Angelica Bell as Ellen Terry in Freshwater, *1935. The photograph was taken in Duncan and Vanessa's studio, which had belonged to Whistler and then Sickert, in Fitzroy Street. 'The play is about Virginia's great-aunt, the photographer Julia Margaret Cameron, the poet Tennyson, the painter G.F. Watts and the actress Ellen Terry who had been married to Watts. In the play she runs away from him with a sailor met on the beach.'*

Words: Quentin Bell; Picture: Tate Gallery Archive

163

Monk's House,
Rodmell,
near Lewes,
Sussex.   17th Aug.

Dearest Christabel,

I never answered your letter; you'll
have understood why I didn't.
The only thing I could do was to be
with Vanessa.   But I did
like your letter, & thank you for
understanding what this means to us.
He was such a joy — with every sort of
gift — & the waste seems unbelievable.
Vanessa seems rather better, but it's
hard to see anyone suffer so much, as you
will understand.
        Thank you again; dearest Christabel
                    Yr Virginia

*Letter to Lady
Aberconway about the
death of Virginia's
nephew, Julian Bell, in
the Spanish Civil War.*

*British Library, Additional
MS 70775, folio 163*

'To Virginia I praised the book more than I should have done if she had been well,' he wrote, in his autobiography. Virginia wrote, 'the moment of relief was divine. I hardly know yet if I'm on my heels or head - so amazing is the reversal... I have never had such an experience before.' She could now begin to work on *Three Guineas* and concentrate more on Roger's biography. She also wrote an article, 'Why Art Today Follows Politics' for the socialist paper, *The Daily Worker*, and to the Memoir Club read a piece called 'Am I a Snob?'.

For once, it was Leonard who was unwell at the beginning of the year, in 1937, and they received dispiriting news of the deaths of Stephen Tomlin, who had sculpted Virginia's head, and Miss West who had managed the Hogarth Press. Leonard recovered quickly, but the following month Virginia's menopausal symptoms and associated feelings of apprehension returned. She dreaded the reviews of *The Years*, which was published in mid-March. When they were favourable, she felt immense relief. The see-saw of emotion continued, however. Julian returned from China only to prepare to leave for Spain, where he intended to fight in the Civil War. At the beginning of April they visited Janet Case, who had remained Virginia's friend from the years of teaching her Greek, and who was now dying. Later the same month, shortly before the Woolfs left to holiday in France, Virginia made the only BBC broadcast that was recorded and remains. All those who knew her have commented on the beauty of her voice; her biographer-nephew, Quentin, commented that the recording captures none of that beauty.

Perhaps its lack of 'depth and resonance' reflected her state of emotional and physical health at the time.

Whilst Leonard and Virginia were touring France in May, they heard that Maynard Keynes was seriously ill. He recovered and they returned, in time for Julian's farewell dinner. He left for Spain, to become a Red Cross ambulance driver rather than a soldier, in early June. That month, *The Years* reached the top of the best-seller list of the *New York Herald Tribune*. During the second week of July, Janet Case's death being imminent, Virginia was asked to prepare an obituary for *The Times*. Janet Case died on 15 July, and on 19 July Virginia wrote an obituary which she thought was 'too stiff & mannered' but which she sent. The next day, before the obituary was published, there came news of another death: Julian's. His ambulance had been shelled in Spain by German planes.

Vanessa was shattered. It was what she had feared and expected, but the news of his death was no more bearable for that. Virginia experienced the double blow of the loss of her nephew and the reaction of her sister. A month after the death, she wrote of her sister, 'now & then she looks an old woman. She reminds me of father taking Thoby's arm: so she asks Q. to help her. How can she ever right herself though?' Virginia's own way of coping was to write a brief memoir of Julian, beginning, 'I am going to set down very quickly what I remember about Julian, - partly because I am too dazed to write what I was writing: &... I know by this time what an odd effect Time has: it does not destroy people... but it brushes away the actual personal presence.'

Their half-brother, Gerald Duckworth, died at the end of September and, in early October, Virginia and Leonard returned to

Angelica, Vanessa and Quentin Bell, 1938.

Tate Gallery Archive

London, having stayed in Sussex since the end of July, giving support to Vanessa. Two days after Virginia returned to London, she finished *Three Guineas*. The title comes from a putative decision the writer has to make: to which three causes should she donate her three guineas? She decides to give them to a women's college rebuilding fund, to a women's employment organization, and to an organization that aims to prevent war. Women's financial independence from men - one theme of *A Room of One's Own* - is central to the arguments presented. She likens the position of women in a patriarchal society to a nation under fascist dictatorship; the private is the political. Virginia's feeling about it, when she received the proofs, was that it 'was like a spine to me all last summer; upheld me in the horror of last August... How can it all have petered out into diluted drivel? But it remains, morally, a spine: the thing I wished to say, though futile.'

Neither Virginia's nor Leonard's health was good, and at the beginning of January 1938 Leonard was in bed for almost two weeks. Then it was Virginia's turn to have a high temperature. She relinquished her share in the Hogarth Press to John Lehmann in March, so that he and Leonard were partners. Later the same month, Hitler invaded Austria, and Virginia wrote, 'the whole of Europe may be in flames - its on the cards'. As the spring settled in, the health of the Woolfs was better, but more old friends died: Ottoline - for whom she wrote *The Times* obituary - in April, and Ka Arnold-Foster (née Cox) in May. Virginia was still writing Roger's biography, but she also had an idea for a novel, provisionally called 'Poyntz Hall'. When *Three Guineas* was published in June, the critics liked it - 'she is the most brilliant pamphleteer in England' - but her friends, on the whole, did not.

Later than usual, in June, Virginia and Leonard took their holiday in Scotland, from where she wrote to Vanessa and Ethel about its beauty. On their return, they spent most of the next three months at Monk's House. In August Virginia, taking a break from writing Roger's biography, noted in her diary, 'The old woman who lived up at Mt Misery drowned herself 3 days ago. The body was found near Piddinghoe - my usual walk... at supper, we discussed our generation: & the prospects of war.' After the Munich crisis at the end of September she wrote, 'The net result is that we are presented with 2 gas masks by the Govt'. The subject of war dominated conversations with friends that autumn and winter, but Virginia remained buoyant:

'pessimism can be routed by getting into the flow: creative writing'. She continued with 'Poyntz Hall' and Roger's biography, wrote 'The Art of Biography' for the *Atlantic Monthly*, and was 'rehashing Lappin & Lapinova', an old story of hers, for *Harper's Bazaar*. On Christmas Eve, Virginia's half-sister Stella's widower, Jack Hills, died. The shadow cast by that news had barely lifted when, the day after Christmas, Leonard's marmoset, Mitzi, also died.

Hitler was inevitably one of the topics of conversation when Virginia and Leonard went to visit the 82-year old Sigmund Freud at the end of January 1939. Freud and his children, Anna and Martin, were recent refugees from Vienna, who now lived in Hampstead, north London. On the day of their visit to Freud, the poet W.B. Yeats died. Virginia was thinking about the achievements of these men and Roger Fry at this time and for the next few months, during which Liverpool University offered her an Honorary Doctorate - despite all that she had written in

Sigmund Freud. Virginia described him in her diary as a 'shrunk very old man: with a monkey's light eyes, paralysed spasmodic movements, inarticulate but alert… an old fire now flickering'

Freud Museum, London

Three Guineas about the necessity of women eschewing such honours. She refused the offer. By early in March, she had finished 'the first sketch of Roger', and having done so was in a receptive frame of mind in mid-April when 'Nessa said that if I did not start writing my memoirs I should soon be too old.' She began them two days later.

The sketch of Roger now had to be polished, and despite 'a little influenza & a cold in the head', she had completed a quarter of it, the first 100 pages, by the end of April. In May, Mark Gertler, a painter who had loved Carrington and known Roger, came to dinner in London. He spoke bitterly of art and literature, and rather dispirited Virginia. But she and Leonard had plans to lift their spirits. They went to Monk's House at the end of the month, from where they travelled to northern France on holiday - less than three months before war was declared. There was no hint of war where they stayed, and they returned refreshed. Two days after they returned, Mark Gertler committed suicide. Four days later, Leonard's mother fell and broke two ribs. She died within a few days. Apart from the 'jading & somehow very depressing' experience of watching her die, Leonard had problems with the publication of his latest book adding to his 'gloom', so that Virginia was 'damnably down in the mouth'. In addition to these emotional upheavals, they were moving to Mecklenburgh Square - not far from their Tavistock Square house, the lease of which they were planning to sell, as a hotel was being built nearby. Nevertheless, at the end of July, as was customary, they went to Monk's House for the summer. The Bloomsbury house-move took place in mid-August, amid an atmosphere of pre-war crisis.

War & Death

On 1 September, Germany invaded Poland, and on the 3rd, England declared war. Virginia and Leonard listened to the Prime Minister's radio announcement in Monk's House. 'My plan is to force my brain to work on Roger. But Lord this is the worst of all my life's experiences.' They remained in the country, travelling to London intermittently, finding the new house chaotic and uncomfortable, and London itself shockingly altered, no longer the place Virginia loved:

> *The City has become merely a congerie of houses lived in by people who work.*
> *There is no society, no luxury no splendour no gadding & flitting. All is serious*
> *& concentrated. It is as if the song had stopped.*

Shaw wrote an article in October, arguing for peace with Hitler, entitled *Uncommon sense about the war*. It caused an outcry: 'Shaw writes an article; Maynard has a heart attack over it; KM an attack of hysteria.' Just before its publication, at the end of September, Freud died. That winter she began reading his work when she found revising her biography of Roger 'a grind'. Virginia began writing journalism again as she and Leonard realized that they would need the money, book sales being uncertain but newspapers always being in demand during war-time. By the end of November she was 'jaded & tired & depressed & cross'. It was an unusually cold and icy winter. At Christmas 1939, it was Angelica's twenty-first birthday, and there was a celebration with family and friends. Virginia was fifty-eight years old. Within two months, despite influenza and bronchitis, she had finished her biography of Roger and awaited assessments of parts of her manuscript from Leonard, Margery Fry and Vanessa. Leonard was uncharacteristically negative, but both Roger's sister and his erstwhile lover felt that Virginia had caught the essence of the man. 'Now you have given him back to me' wrote Vanessa, and Margery wrote, 'it's *him*'.

When Virginia's health had improved, Vita spent two days at Monk's House at the end of April, shortly before Virginia gave a talk on Freud to the Workers' Education Association in Brighton. In the middle of May, having heard a radio broadcast on defence against parachutists, Virginia and Leonard 'discussed suicide if

Hitler lands. Jews beaten up. What point in waiting?'. Despite this 'matter of fact talk', Virginia continued to write 'Poyntz Hall' and replied affectionately to a letter from Shaw in which he had written of an encounter Roger Fry had had with Sir Edward Elgar, and which she quoted in her biography of Roger. In mid-June, Paris was invaded and Prime Minister Churchill broadcast on the radio: 'Reassuring about defence of England; not all claptrap. Now we're fighting alone with our back to the wall.' The Woolfs had more friends to stay at Monk's House, amongst them the writer Elizabeth Bowen, with whom the Woolfs had stayed in Ireland. Virginia corrected the proofs of her biography, wrote her novel and continued with her memoirs of the family. The 1910 Dreadnought Hoax was the subject of a talk she gave to the local Women's Institute in July, a couple of days before *Roger Fry: A Biography* was published.

'Poyntz Hall' absorbed more and more of her interest as the summer went on. Set in the summer, in the grounds and interior of a country house, it centres on a marriage, and a pageant of English history, enacted by ordinary people under the direction of a Miss La Trobe, and watched by an audience, many of whom misunderstand much of it. For a moment, however, the work of art that is created gives order to the chaos of human life. As Virginia wrote her novel, the Battle of Britain raged. Germany began a bombing offensive, initially against coastal shipping. The bombing was then directed inland to southern England, especially Sussex, Kent and London. Towards the end of August, the focus became aircraft factories and airfields, and then British cities. Night-time bombing began in October.

Roger's biography sold well in the midst of the terror. Virginia's August diary entries comment on both the sales and the bombardment:

Large air flights – little white gnats this evening. Sales very good – 2nd edition ordered. But I want sleep & silence.

Third edition ordered… Many air raids. One as I walked. A haystack was handy. But walked on, & so home. All clear. Then sirens again.

They came very close. We lay down under a tree... We lay flat on our faces, hands behind head. Don't close yr teeth said L... Bombs shook the windows of my lodge. Will it drop I asked? If so, we shall be broken together. I thought, I think, of nothingness – flatness, my mood being flat. Some fear I suppose. Shd we take Mabel to garage. Too risky to cross the garden L. said. Then another came from Newhaven. Hum & saw & buzz all round us. A horse neighed in the marsh. My books only gave me pain, Ch. Brontë said. Today I agree... The all clear... 144 down last night.

Book flopped. Sales down to 15 a day since air raid on London. Is that the reason? Will it pick up?

In early September, Mecklenburgh Square was bombed, but their house remained standing, although a second explosion less than a week later meant that 'all our windows are broken, ceilings down, & most of our china smashed'. The press was moved north of London to Letchworth in Hertfordshire. Less than a month later:

John says Tavistock Sqre is no more... Second, an urgent request from Harpers Bazaar for an article or story... the effort has its reward; for I'm worth, owing to that insect like conscience & diligence, £120 to the USA... The light is now fading. Soon the Siren; then the twang of plucked strings... But its almost forgettable still; the nightly operation on the tortured London.

But life in London went on - even at the London Library, where it was decided that Virginia should be proposed for the committee. E.M. Forster, who had five years before 'sniffed about women on Cttee', put the proposal to her. Her response was, 'No. I don't want to be a sop - a face saver.' In Sussex, two weeks later she had finished her novel:

am a little triumphant about the book. I think it is an interesting attempt in a new method. I think it is more quintessential than the others. More milk

The back view of Monk's House today, showing Virginia's ground-floor bedroom extension.

skimmed off. A richer pat, certainly a fresher than that misery The Years. I've enjoyed writing almost every page.

This equilibrium was upset by a land mine at the back of Mecklenburgh Square 'killing several families and blasting all our rooms in reverse direction from the previous bombing', wrote Leonard, in his autobiography. 'You could stand on the ground floor and look up with uninterrupted view to the roof.' From beneath the rubble, books and furniture were salvaged and removed to Monk's House, which became 'gorged with old jugs & lidless pots. And the Christian room laden with 4 tons of old damp books. Real life is a helter skelter, healthy for the mind doubtless', Virginia wrote in her diary. Now they would live full-time in the country. When once she had explored the streets of London after a morning's writing and lunch, she now walked on the Sussex Downs and by the river, sometimes with their spaniel, Sally, sometimes alone. On her long walks she mulled over her writing and, now redrafting

*Virginia's affectionate
letter to Shaw, prompted
by his sending her a
letter containing an
account of Roger Fry's
meeting the composer
Sir Edward Elgar.
Shaw's letter had ended
by referring to when
'I'd first met you and, of
course, fell in love with
you. I suppose every man
did'.*

British Library Additional
MS 50522, folio 293

*In relation to Virginia's
biography of Roger Fry,
Shaw gave her a picture
of a Fry landscape. She
sent him a postcard of
Monk's House, with
thanks.*

British Library Additional
MS 50522, folio 318

> Monk's House,
> Rodmell,
> near Lewes,
> Sussex.
>
> 15th May 1940
>
> Dear Mr Shaw,
>
> Your letter reduced me to two days silence from sheer pleasure. You wont be surprised to hear that I promptly lifted some paragraphs and inserted them in my proofs. You may take what action you like.
>
> As for the falling in love, it was not, let me confess, one-sided. When I first met you at the Webbs I was set against all great men, having been liberally fed on them in my father's house. I wanted only to meet business men and (say) racing experts. But in a jiffy you made me re-consider all that and had me at your feet. Indeed you have acted a lover's part in my life for the past thirty years; and though I daresay its not much to boast of, I should have been a worser woman without Bernard Shaw. That is the reason--I mean the multiplicity of your lovers and what you must suffer from them-- why Leonard and Virginia have never liked to impose themselves upon you. But we have an intermittent perch--37 Mecklenburgh Square-- in London; and if ever Mr Shaw dropped his handkerchief-- to recur to the love theme-- we should ask nothing better than to come and see you.
>
> As for the Roger Fry picture, I should accept it gratefully. For that offer, and for your letter, and for everything else that you have given me, I am always yours humbly and gratefully,
>
> *Virginia Woolf*
>
> Heartbreak House, by the way, is my favourite of all your works.

293

The address for the picture is.
Hogarth Press
37 Mecklenburgh
Square.
WC 1.
This is our Monk
House on the back
and thanks.

Virginia Woolf

G. Bernard Shaw
4 Whitehall Court
(130)
London
SW 1.

318

Monk's House
Rodmell
near Lewes
Sussex

26ᵗʰ Sept 40.

Dearest Christabel,

Your letter went first to Tavistock Square, which we have left, & then to Mecklenburgh Square, where our flat — 37 — has just been partly destroyed in an air raid. But wasn't read on till a day or two ago. I cant therefore see Lord Briceter, but have written to explain. What on earth can Lord Bricter want to talk to me about? I cant imagine any connection between him & Roger Fry. Once I did know an undergraduate called John Hugh Smith, & vaguely remember a large house in Putney. However, I hope he'll explain: a trust I'm not to be imprisoned for libel.

I hope you're not staying in London — And in the vast house with the lift in which I ascended innumerable flights to a bedroom about the size of the Round Pond in

which — do you remember? — there was a child with a Balmoral wheel — has it vanished? Is Grosvenor Square just as palatial? Shall we ever meet again?

Well anyhow it was very nice to meet via the mysterious Lord Bricter whom I somehow suspect of being a German spy.

And Leonard returns your superior brand of love.

(I noted that mine was only love: his best — oh dear! —

temperately

but your husband
lovingly
Virginia Woolf.

Letter from Virginia to Lady Aberconway about the bombing of the Woolfs' London home in 1940. The tone is buoyant and, ironically, she asks, 'Shall we ever meet again?'- six months before her suicide.

British Library, Additional MS 70775, folios 164 and 164 verso

'Poyntz Hall', she also worked on stories and a history of literature.

Shortly before Christmas, Virginia matter-of-factly outlined in her diary the privations of war then commented, 'We are of course marooned here by the bombs in London... The Germans are said to be sending troops to occupy the recumbent Italy. Whats Hitler got up his sleeve next? - we ask. A certain old age feeling sometimes makes me think I cant spend force as I used. And my hand shakes. Otherwise we draw breath as usual.' Despite the bombs in London, Virginia and Leonard went there early in January 1941, where she 'wandered in the desolate ruins of my old squares: gashed; dismantled; the old red bricks all white powder, something like a builders yard. Grey dirt & broken windows; sightseers; all that completeness ravished & demolished.' Two weeks later she was writing, 'This trough of despair shall not, I swear, engulf me', and in another two weeks: 'Why was I depressed? I cannot remember.'

Working on her non-fiction and seeing friends and family lifted her spirits. She and Leonard went to London twice more, and then on to Cambridge, where they visited Pernel Strachey at Newnham and Dadie Rylands at King's College: 'I like the dinner with Dadie best. All very lit up & confidential. I like the soft grey night at Newnham.' On their way home, they visited the press in Letchworth and, once home, she had finished 'Poyntz Hall' within ten days, and decided to call it 'Between the Acts'. In the same diary entry as she noted this, at the end of February, she recorded her disgust at women she overheard talking in Brighton. She called them 'common little tarts', and another two women, whom she observed stuffing themselves with food and talking of their plenty at home, she described as 'fat white slugs'. At the beginning of March she determined to avoid introspection and instead observe: 'Observe the oncome of age. Observe greed. Observe my own despondency. By that means it becomes serviceable. Or so I hope. I insist upon spending this time to the best advantage. I will go down with my colours flying... Occupation is essential... the sight of Oxford Street & Piccadilly (which) haunt me. Oh dear yes, I shall conquer this mood.' But she did not.

Virginia now felt that 'Between the Acts' was worthless and could not be published. Leonard recorded in his own diary his concern for Virginia's health. He asked Vanessa to come to tea, letting her know his worries about Virginia. She was sufficiently unsettled to write Virginia a note when she got home. In it, she thanked Virginia for all the support she had been given by her since Julian's death, emphasizing the strength her sister gave her. She also told her, in her elder sister tone, 'you must not go and get ill just now'. Virginia was, at the same time, writing a letter - to John Lehmann, sending him the 'Between the Acts' typescript and expressing her low estimation of its worth but asking him to decide if it was worth publishing. Her reply to her sister was not to be sent, but found:

Dearest,

You can't think how I loved your letter. But I feel that I have gone too far this time to come again. I am certain now that I am going mad again. It is just as it was the first time, I am always hearing voices, and I know I shant get over it now.

All I want to say is that Leonard has been so astonishingly good, every day, always; I cant imagine that anyone could have done more for me than he has. We have been perfectly happy until the last few weeks, when this horror began. Will you assure him of this? I feel he has so much to do that he will go on, better without me, and you will help him.

I can hardly think clearly any more. If I could I would tell you what you and the children have meant to me. I think you know.

I have fought against it, but I cant any longer.

Virginia

This was dated 'Sunday', presumably 23 March 1941. Virginia kept the letter hidden, as she did two of a similar sort to Leonard. On the Monday, she received an enthusiastic letter from John Lehmann, who wished to publish *Between the Acts*. Her frame of mind was unaltered, and Leonard was very concerned. On the Wednesday, at his wits' end, he telephoned Octavia Wilberforce, a doctor and friend whom Virginia trusted, for an appointment to see her with Virginia in Brighton. Although unwell herself, Dr Wilberforce readily agreed and an appointment was made for the next day. Before leaving for the afternoon appointment on the Thursday, Virginia

The Hogarth Press

John Lehmann   Leonard Woolf

37, Mecklenburgh Square, London, w.c.1.

Telephone: Terminus 7545.   Cables: Hogarth London.

28/3/41

Dear John,

       I enclose a letter from Virginia. The fact is that she is on the verge of a complete nervous break down and is seriously ill. The war, food &c have been telling on her and I have seen it coming on for some time. It is out of the question for her to touch the book now and so we must put it off indefinitely. Send it back to me and <u>dont answer this letter</u>. I will come up to town and discuss the whole thing with you when I can. I am sorry for your and the Press sake; there seems some fate against you in the publishing world. The whole thing is a nightmare. Would you mind writing a note to V saying that you're very sorry that we shant be able to publish in the spring, but that we we will hope for the autumn?

     Yours

Leonard Woolf

Monks House Rodmell Lewes

28/3/41   3

Dear John,

       I'd decided, before your letter came, that I cant publish that novel as it stands-- its too silly and trivial.

       What I will do is to revise it, and see if I can pull it together and so publish it in the au tumn. If published as it is, it would certainly mean a financial loss; which we dont want. I am sure I am right about this.

       I ne dnt say how sorry I am to have troubled you. The fact is it was written in the intervals of doing Roger with my brain half asleep. And I didnt realise how bad it was till I read it over

       Please forgive me, and believe I'm only doing what is best.

      I'm sending back the Mss. with my notes.

       Again, I apologise profoundly.

     Yours

Virginia Woolf

Letters to John Lehmann about Between the Acts *from Virginia and Leonard.*

British Library, Additional MS 56234, folios 2 and 3

wrote a reply to John Lehmann, telling him not to publish her novel. She wished to revise it, she wrote. She gave the letter to Leonard, who enclosed it with a covering letter explaining that Virginia was 'on the verge of a complete nervous break down and (is) seriously ill'.

Although Virginia liked Octavia Wilberforce, she gave the impression of being extremely annoyed at the pointless examination the doctor wished to make, but she submitted. Memories of enforced 'rest cures' from her powerless past caused Virginia to ask Octavia not to order one now. Gently, Octavia asked Virginia to trust her judgment - that Virginia should rest. Virginia and Leonard returned home and, in the evening, listened to the BBC broadcast of Beethoven's 'Appassionata' Sonata. Leonard was relieved that Virginia's spirits seemed to have lifted. The next morning - Friday, 28 March 1941 - after half-heartedly giving their servant, Louie, some help with the dusting, Virginia walked out to her writing lodge. Leonard brought her back into the house at about 11am. In the sitting room, probably before she walked once again to the lodge, Virginia left her earlier letter to Vanessa and this letter to Leonard, dated 'Tuesday':

Dearest,

I feel certain that I am going mad again: I feel we cant go through another of those terrible times. And I shant recover this time. I begin to hear voices, and cant concentrate. So I am doing what seems the best thing to do. You have given me the greatest possible happiness. You have been in every way all that anyone could be. I dont think two people could have been happier till this terrible disease came. I cant fight it any longer, I know that I am spoiling your life, that without me you could work. And you will I know. You see I cant even write this properly. I cant read. What I want to say is that I owe all the happiness of my life to you. You have been entirely patient with me and incredibly good. I want to say that - everybody knows it. If anybody could have saved me it would have been you. Everything has gone from me but the certainty of your goodness. I cant go on spoiling your life any longer.

I dont think two people could have been happier than we have been.

V.

Having gone out to the writing lodge again, Virginia returned to the house for her fur coat and walking stick before walking towards the river. There she found a large stone, put it into her pocket and stepped or threw herself off the bank into the river. In her Lodge she had left another, undated letter for Leonard:

Dearest,

I want to tell you that you have given me complete happiness. No one could have done more than you have done. Please believe that.

But I know that I shall never get over this: and I am wasting your life. It is this madness. Nothing anyone says can persuade me. You can work, and you will be much better without me. You see I cant write this even, which shows I am right. All I want to say is that until this disease came on we were perfectly happy. It was all due to you. No one could have been so good as you have been, from the very first day till now. Everyone knows that.

V.

You will find Roger's letter to the Maurons in the writing table drawer in the Lodge. Will you destroy all my papers.

At 1pm, Leonard left his study, intending to listen to the news in the sitting room before having lunch. He saw the letters, read the one addressed to him, and raced downstairs to ask Louie if she had seen his wife leave the house. He told her that he thought something had happened to her, and then ran to look for Virginia in the lodge, the garden and then by the river. Very soon he saw her stick floating in the river, and Virginia's footprints on the bank. The police arrived and searched the river and the surrounding countryside, as did Leonard. After four days, there was still no sign of her. As Leonard had informed Vanessa, John Lehmann and Vita of Virginia's disappearance and suicide notes, he thought it necessary to prevent rumour spreading, and wrote to the editor of *The Times*, telling him what had happened. On Wednesday 3 April, a notice appeared in *The Times*: 'it must now be presumed that Mrs Leonard Woolf (Virginia Woolf, the novelist and essayist), who has been missing since last Friday, has been drowned in the Sussex Ouse at Rodmell, near

Lewes.' There was also a five paragraph obituary. The same evening, the BBC radio news included the announcement of her death. Her body had still not been found.

After tributes from friends had been written in national newspapers, local newspapers had reported the 'unavailing search', and hundreds of people had written letters to Leonard, three weeks after Virginia had walked out of Monk's House, her body was found by a teenage boy who was cycling with group of friends. They had seen a mysterious object in the river, had thrown stones to get it to the bank and discovered it was the fur-coated body of Virginia. Her watch had stopped at 11.45.

'Leonard has been so astonishingly good, every day, always… he has so much to do that he will go on better without me'.

Random House, London

≫ *Between the Acts & After*

My first memory... is the most important of all my memories. If life has a base that it stands upon, if it is a bowl that one fills and fills and fills - then my bowl without a doubt stands upon this memory. It is of lying half asleep, the waves breaking, one, two, one, two, and sending a splash of water over the beach; and then breaking, one, two, one, two, behind a yellow blind. It is of hearing the blind draw its little acorn across the floor as the wind blew the blind out. It is of lying and hearing this splash and seeing this light, and feeling, it is almost impossible that I should be here; of feeling the purest ecstasy I can conceive.

A Sketch of the Past

After the inquest, Virginia's body was cremated and Leonard buried her ashes in the garden of Monk's House, under an elm tree. The tree no longer stands, but marking her grave is an inscription, quoting the last words of her novel, *The Waves*:

Against you I will fling myself, unvanquished and unyielding, O Death!

Virginia's last novel, *Between the Acts*, was published posthumously. Leonard lived until 1969, and left Monk's House to the National Trust, which keeps it open to visitors. He tried to ensure that Virginia's literary remains - her manuscripts, typescripts and diaries - were held together in one 'first-rate' place of learning. In this, he was not wholly successful, and in many ways this is fortunate. Virginia's manuscripts, typescripts and corrected proofs may be examined by scholars in a number of places in England and the United States. Her reputation and popularity have fluctuated, but scholars have continued to find new things to observe and comment upon in her work-in-progress. Perhaps the greatest of her works is her diary, the full text of which is available in five paperback volumes. Many biographies of her have been written. Her image appears on an incongruous variety of commercial items. She is a feminist icon and her works are to be found on the syllabus of any place of higher learning where literature is studied. Was she a snob? Was she a radical? Was she a socialist or an elitist? Fortunately, all her works are in print, so we may each judge for ourselves.

Opposite page:

The sculptured head of Virginia Woolf, made by Stephen Tomlin in 1931, and the plaque bearing the quotation from The Waves.

National Trust/Eric Crichton

VIRGINIA WOOLF *1882-1941*

≈ *Chronology*

1878	26 March: Julia Duckworth, mother of George, Stella and Gerald, marries Leslie Stephen, father of Laura
1879	30 May: Vanessa Stephen is born to Julia and Leslie Stephen
1880	8 September: Julian Thoby Stephen is born
1882	25 January: Adeline Virginia Stephen is born at 22 Hyde Park Gate
1883	27 October: Adrian Leslie Stephen is born
1889	Madge Symonds stays at 22 Hyde Park Gate
1891	The *Hyde Park Gate News* is first produced by the Stephen children
1895	5 May: mother's death; Virginia experiences her first mental breakdown
1897	19 July: Stella's death three months after her marriage; Virginia attends Greek and history classes at King's College, London
1899	Thoby Stephen enters Trinity College, Cambridge, and meets Clive Bell, Saxon Sydney-Turner, Lytton Strachey and Leonard Woolf
1900	Virginia and Vanessa go to the Trinity College May Ball
1902	Virginia begins lessons with Janet Case; Virginia's father becomes Sir Leslie Stephen
1904	22 February: father's death; Violet Dickinson cares for Virginia during her nervous breakdown; George Duckworth marries; Virginia's first articles are published
1905	Virginia teaches at Morley College; 'Thursday Evenings' begin at 46 Gordon Square
1906	22 November: Thoby's death; Vanessa accepts Clive Bell's proposal of marriage
1907	Vanessa marries Clive Bell; Virginia and Adrian move to 29 Fitzroy Square
1908	Vanessa's first son, Julian Bell is born at 46 Gordon Square

1909   Lytton Strachey proposes to Virginia; Virginia meets Ottoline Morrell

1910   The Dreadnought Hoax; Virginia is unwell; Quentin Bell is born at
46 Gordon Square

1911   Leonard Woolf returns from Ceylon; Virginia and Leonard meet at
the Bells' house

1912   Virginia takes a rest cure and sees a psychologist; she marries Leonard Woolf
in August

1913   Virginia's mental distress leads to a suicide attempt; she is cared for by nurses

1914   Virginia's health improves; war is declared; the Woolfs move to Richmond

1915   Virginia begins a diary; her mental health worsens; *The Voyage Out*
is published by Duckworth; the Woolfs move to Hogarth House
in Richmond

1916   Virginia begins a friendship with Katherine Mansfield; Vanessa moves
to Charleston

1917   The Woolfs buy a printing press: they publish *The Mark on the Wall*
and *Three Jews*

1918   The Woolfs decline publishing James Joyce's *Ulysses*; an armistice
is declared; Angelica Bell, daughter of Vanessa and Duncan Grant, is born
on Christmas Day

1919   T.S. Eliot's *Poems* is published by Hogarth Press; the Woolfs buy
Monk's House; *Night and Day* is published by Duckworth

1920   The first meeting of the Memoir Club; the last meeting of Virginia and
Katherine Mansfield

1921   Virginia experiences 'all the horrors of the dark cupboard of illness'
in the summer

1922   *Jacob's Room* published by Hogarth Press; Virginia meets Vita Sackville-West

1923   9 January: death of Katherine Mansfield; Hogarth Press publishes
The Waste Land

1924   Woolfs move to 52 Tavistock Square; *Mr Bennett and Mrs Brown* is published

1925   *Mrs Dalloway* and *The Common Reader* are published; Virginia and Vita
are together at Long Barn

1926 The General Strike; the Woolfs visit Thomas Hardy; Virginia has 'a whole nervous breakdown in miniature' in July

1927 *To the Lighthouse* is published; the Woolfs buy their first car

1928 *Orlando* is published; Virginia travels with Vita Sackville-West in France

1929 *A Room of One's Own* is published

1930 Friendship begins with Ethel Smyth; Virginia's 'brush with death'

1931 *The Waves* is published; Virginia sits for a sculpture of her head and shoulders

1932 Lytton Strachey dies; *The Common Reader: Second Series* is published

1933 *Flush* is published; Virginia declines an honorary doctorate from Manchester University

1934 Roger Fry dies; Virginia agrees to write his biography

1935 *Freshwater* is performed; the Woolfs travel in Europe by car

1936 Virginia is unwell for much of the year; she neglects her diary

1937 *The Years* is published; Julian Bell is killed in Spain

1938 *Three Guineas* is published; Ottoline Morrell dies

1939 Virginia declines an honorary doctorate from Liverpool University; the Woolfs move to Mecklenburgh Square and travel in France; war is declared

1940 *Roger Fry: A Biography* is published; the Woolfs' London home is bombed; the Hogarth Press moves

1941 28 March: Virginia commits suicide; *Between the Acts* is published posthumousl

FURTHER READING

Quentin Bell

Virginia Woolf: A Biography

The Hogarth Press, 1982

James King

Virginia Woolf

Hamish Hamilton, 1994

Hermione Lee

Virginia Woolf

Chatto & Windus, 1996

Nigel Nicolson, ed.

The Letters of Virginia Woolf: Volumes 1-6

Hogarth Press, 1974-80

Joan Russell Noble, ed.

Recollections of Virginia Woolf

Peter Owen, 1972

Panthea Reid

Art and Affection: A Life of Virginia Woolf

Oxford University Press, 1996

Leonard Woolf

Sowing, Growing, Beginning Again,
Downhill All the Way, The Journey not the Arrival Matters
five volumes of autobiography

Hogarth Press, 1962-9

Andrew McNiellie & Anne Olivier Bell eds.

The Diary of Virginia Woolf: Volumes 1-5

Hogarth Press, 1977-1984

A page from the typescript of 'A Sketch of the Past' *in which Virginia Woolf reflects on the closeness of her relationship with her sister in 'that world of men'.*

British Library, Additional MS 61973, folio 54

122   54

(15th Nov. 1940)

We never spoke, during those unhappy years, of those

scenes. (Scenes, I note, seldom illustrate my relation with

Vanessa; it has been too deep for scenes) Thoby, I imagine,

never guessed at thxxix their existnce. He may have had a

vague conception that something as he would have put it,

was 'up' between Jack and Vanessa. But his gneral attidtue

was aloof--was he not a man? Did not men ignore domestic

trifles?---and judicial. From his remote station, as school

boy, as undergraduate, he felt gnerally speaking that

we should accept our lot; if George wanted us to go to

parties, why not? If father --who was not, he once told me,

a normal specimen of manhood-- wished us to walk , we should.

Once at Salisbury when the Fishers were neighbours, Vanessa,

destroing them, and in particualr Aunt Mary, who had

viciously interfered, writing surroptious letters addressed

to Copes studio, criticing her behaviour toawrds George and

Jack, --when Vanessa refused to visit them, and cut them

in the street, Thoby pronounced one of his rare impressive

judgments. He said gruffly it was not right to treat Aunt

Mary like that.

        It thus came about that Nessa and I formed together

a close conspiracy. In that world of many men, coming and

going, in that big house of innumerable rooms, we formed our

private muclues. I visulaise it as a little sensitive

centre of acute life; of instantaeous sympathy, in the

great echoing shell of Hyde Park Gate.   The shell

was empjty all day. In the evening back they would all come;

Adrain from Westminster; Jack from Lincolns Inn Fields;

FLUSH
A BIOGRAPHY
Virginia Woolf

JACOB'S ROOM

VIRGINIA WOOLF

MRS. DALLOWAY

VIRGINIA WOOLF

THE VO

VIRGIN

PUBLISHED BY LEONARD AND VIRGINIA WOOLF AT THE
HOGARTH PRESS, 52 TAVISTOCK SQUARE, LONDON, W.C.

1933

PUBLISHED BY LEONARD & VIRGINIA
WOOLF AT THE HOGARTH PRESS,
TAVISTOCK SQUARE. LONDON. 1929.

THE
COMMON READER

VIRGINIA WOOLF

PUBLISHED BY LEONARD & VIRGINIA
WOOLF AT THE HOGARTH PRESS,
TAVISTOCK SQUARE. LONDON, 1929.

T

PUBLISHED BY L
WOOLF AT TH
TAVISTOCK SQU

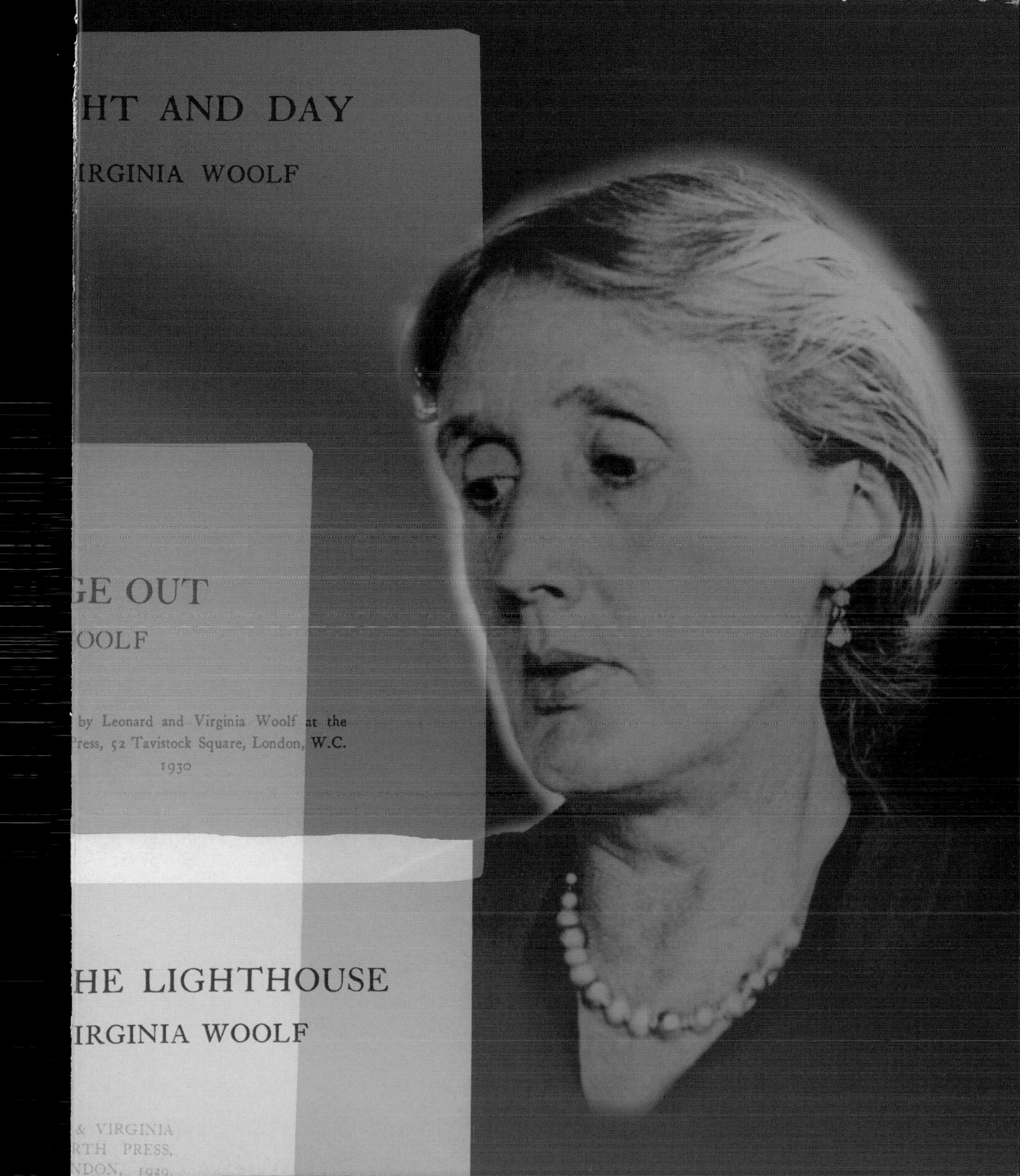
HT AND DAY
IRGINIA WOOLF
GE OUT
OOLF
by Leonard and Virginia Woolf at the
Press, 52 Tavistock Square, London, W.C.
1930
HE LIGHTHOUSE
IRGINIA WOOLF
& VIRGINIA
RTH PRESS,

Index

The British Library is grateful to the following for permission to reproduce illustrations: the Tate Gallery Archive, the Executors of the Virginia Woolf Estate and the Hogarth Press as publisher, reprinted with permission by the Random House Group Limited; the National Portrait Gallery, London; Dr Milo Keynes; King's College Library, Cambridge; Glasgow Museums: Art Gallery and Museum, Kelvingrove; Freud Museum, London/Sigmund Freud Copyrights; The Lilly Library, Indiana University, Bloomington, Indiana.

Front cover: Portrait of Virginia Woolf, painted by Vanessa Bell, circa 1912 (National Trust/Eric Crichton); the manuscript of *Mrs Dalloway* (British Library, Additional MS 51044, folio 124); Fitzroy Square (photographer unknown).

Back cover: Detail from a photograph of Virginia Stephen with Stella and George Duckworth, taken in 1896 (Tate Gallery Archive); the back view of Monk's House today, showing Virginia Woolf's ground floor corner bedroom (National Trust/Eric Crichton).

Half-title page: Undated photograph of Virginia Woolf taken by Leonard Woolf in Monk's House (Sussex University Library: Leonard Woolf Papers Ad. 26).

Frontispiece: Letter from Virginia Woolf to Pernel Strachey (British Library, Additional MS 60734, folios 159, 159 verso, 160 and 160 verso).

Contents page: Talland House/Godrevy Lighthouse today (courtesy of William Heller, Digital Imagemakers, St Ives).

Text Copyright: © 2000 Ruth Webb
Illustrations Copyright: © 2000 The British Library Board,
and other named copyright holders

Published in the United States of America by
Oxford University Press, Inc.
198 Madison Avenue
New York, NY 10016

Oxford is a registered trademark of Oxford University Press, Inc.

ISBN 0-19-521559-1

First published 2000 by The British Library, 96 Euston Road, London NW1 2DB

Map by John Mitchell
Designed and typeset by Crayon Design, Stoke Row, Henley-on-Thames
Colour and black-and-white origination by Crayon Design and South Sea International Press
Printed in Hong Kong by South Sea International Press